Flow-based Leadership

**What the Best Firefighters Can Teach You about Leadership and
Making Hard Decisions**

Judith L. Glick-Smith, Ph.D.

Technics Publications

Published by:

2 Lindsley Road
Basking Ridge, NJ 07920 USA

https://www.technicspub.com

Cover design by John Fiorentino and edited by Judi Hopson

First Printing 2016

Copyright © 2016 by Judith L. Glick-Smith, Ph.D.

ISBN, print ed.   9781634621342
ISBN, Kindle ed.   9781634621359
ISBN, ePub ed.   9781634621366
ISBN, Audio ed.   9781634621380

Library of Congress Control Number: 2016944027

To Kieki, Jordan, and Hannah

Table of Contents

Acknowledgements

I will begin with my initial thanks to my brother-in-law, Retired Battalion Chief Steven Strawderman, who shared his decision making story with me, and then proceeded to introduce me to his amazing friends in the fire service.

Steve's friends led me to other members of the fire service, who became participants in my doctoral study, all of whom I thank for their participation and their willingness to allow me to retell their stories in this book.

It was this snowball effect that led me to Battalion Chief David Rhodes, who graciously opened the door to the Georgia Smoke Diver (GSD) program to me. Chief Rhodes has been an amazing collaborator in my efforts to complete this book. I will be forever grateful for the many, many discussions we have had over the years and for his willingness to share his knowledge. The men and women of GSD have been my world for the last five years. I have been honored to have the opportunity to hang out, observe, participate in various deep (and not-so-deep) discussions, and listen to their stories.

These connections have led me to observe other training programs, including Fire Fighter Weekend (at the Georgia Public Safety Training Center), AXIOMS of Leadership, and Georgia F.L.A.M.E.S. In fact, thanks to the encouragement of Fire Chief Michael Baxter, I actually completed the life-changing AXIOMS class.

I'm grateful for long conversations with people like David Wall (Division Director, Georgia Fire Academy), who is in the throes of writing his own dissertation on decision making, Retired Fire Chief Phil Chovan (GSD #84), and Chief of the Fire Asylum Marty Mayes.

There are also all my friends within the profession of technical communication and the world of business, like Thomas Koulopoulos and Michael Rochelle, who have offered their words of encouragement. Then, there was De Murr, who cooked for me while I wrote, when we were working a project together in Philadelphia a few years ago. I would be highly remiss leaving out my Starbucks cohorts, Eddie Sayer, Brad Banyas, Mike Dunn, Gianni and Ann Louise Bonnani, and all the baristas at the Brookwood and GA-141 store, who have kindly spent countless hours listening to me process all this information verbally. In fact, it was Eddie who led me to Steve Hoberman, the best editor and publisher a new author could ever ask for.

An endeavor, such as this, really does involve many people. The connections have occurred almost magically and at exactly the right moments in time. Thanks to all who have cheered me on over the years.

Judith L. Glick-Smith, Ph.D.

Foreword

There is so much that we don't know about how and why we make the decisions we make when we are under stress. Until I met Miss Judy, I had never heard the term "flow" in my studies on decision making. As we met and discussed the concepts of consciousness and connectivity to a situation, I immediately knew what she was talking about, but just didn't know that it had a name. While I can definitively say that I don't think I will ever completely understand the dynamic processes of the mind, opening up my experiences and the Georgia Smoke Diver program to a person who looked at our program through a completely different lens has added value and connected another couple of dots on why things work the way they do within our organization.

Storytelling is the most ancient form of communicating lessons and learning from one another. In our modern world of emojis, it is interesting to take a glimpse into what could only be described as peeling a layer off of, and starting to make sense of, where art meets science when it comes to critical decision making, team leadership, self-development, and awareness. First-hand accounts of some of the nation's most recognized incidents, along with incidents that have become routine, help us gain perspective and learn from the experiences, successes, and failures of others.

The flow of something can be described as the path something takes based on the influences and circumstances of the environment. Water naturally flows downhill because of gravity. It flows out of a firefighter's nozzle in a specific direction, if forced under pressure, until that pressure dissipates and then it's back to gravity. The heat from a fire rises based on the laws of physics until there is a barrier, and then it travels from high pressure to low pressure in and out of a structure fire. So, what is the "flow" of our decision making process, and how can that be applied to leadership?

Understanding why we do what we do is the first step in designing training programs, establishing policy, communicating ideas with others, and understanding ourselves. Opening up the discussion of Flow-based Leadership ties together and gives a name to something that we all know is there, but maybe didn't fully understand, much like the recent "Flow Path" studies within the fire service. It is something we all knew was there, but just never acknowledged it as a specific thing. It was just what happened based on convection currents.

I am very fortunate to be in a career that allows you to see the absolute worst and best of things and people on a regular basis. It has led me to an interesting process of matching up resources to solve problems. Matching the right person, who has the right talent and passion to resolve the problem, with the victim or person with the problem to solve results in both receiving the same satisfaction for different reasons. Our journey with Miss Judy is no different. From a kitchen table conversation in an attempt to help her with doctoral research for opening up the secret society of the Georgia Smoke Divers, she has now delivered back to us an understanding of what the "magic" is and why things work in our world.

David Rhodes
Battalion Chief
City of Atlanta Fire Rescue Department

GSD #339 and Smoke Daddy #5
Georgia Smoke Diver

Logistics Section Chief
Fire Department Instructors Conference
Hands On Training Coordinator

Introduction

"For unless one is able to live fully in the present, the future is a hoax."

—Alan Watts

September 11, 2001 began as a glorious morning. The sky over New York City was clear, a cloudless lapis blue. Joel Kanasky, a firefighter for the New York City Fire Department (FDNY) Rescue Company 1, was teaching a scuba diving class when he heard about the first plane hitting the World Trade Center. As he made his way downtown, he could see the smoke and flames breaching the beautiful sky. He watched, horrified, along with the rest of us as the South Tower fell. He arrived at the site around forty minutes after his company deployed.

He entered the lobby of the North Tower looking for his crew. He approached a battalion chief—according to Joel, "a tough old Marine-coot"—who died later that day when the North Tower fell. The chief gave Joel an order to get some hydraulic jacks and torches, because there were steel beams pinning firefighters in the fallen rubble.

Joel and two other firefighters were getting the equipment together when they heard people yelling, "*RUN!!!*" He didn't even think about it. He dropped all the gear except one tool, and took off across West Street. He found a door and broke its window. He dove through, dropping to his hands and knees. He took the first left into what turned out to be the ATM lobby in the North Tower of the World Trade Center. Joel crawled to a back corner, where he thought his life was going to end. He was totally encapsulated, in what he called "some crazy dust."

He thought about all the young, new firefighters he had trained over the years and how he told them, as he guided them through their training, "Keep your head. Keep breathing. Stay low. Calm down. Slow down. It will be fine." He said he thought these were odd things to think about, but it worked like magic and helped him stay calm.

There was another firefighter, named Thor, with him. Joel didn't have a breathing apparatus because his original task was to get rescue equipment. Thor had one, but there was so much debris in his face piece that he couldn't breathe through it.

He heard Thor say in resignation, "This is probably it." At that moment, Joel saw a touch of light toward the end of the hallway. He said, "We have to crawl that way." They crawled out of the ATM lobby into the back of the American Express Building, where there was enough fresh air to breathe, but he still believed this was probably the end.

Joel felt no sense of time that day. While 47 minutes had passed between the collapse of the South Tower and the collapse of the North Tower, it felt like it was a blink of an eye. His first awareness of the passing of time was at sunset, when he noticed a man cutting bologna and making sandwiches with a loaf of white bread and a big jar of mustard on a garbage can. He said it felt as if he had just entered the North Tower lobby.

I asked Joel what he thought got him through that day. Joel's observation was that training and preparation give you the ability to respond the right way, without regard to time constraints. He understands the value of repetition during training, which helps us make decisions that enable us to remain fully in the present.

Joel was one of 11 survivors of FDNY Rescue Company 1 that fateful day. Joel continued to serve as a firefighter until 2015, when he finally retired. He loved his job at a level few of us can imagine. He worked in a special operations company in New York City, where his primary function was to save firefighters. In a 2010 interview, he told me,

> "That's my responsibility. We're there when firemen get in trouble. I've been to many firefighter fatality rooms in twenty years. It's been tough duty, but by the same token, we pulled out fifteen or so who are still alive today... [Being a firefighter] was always a desire and a love. I thought it was a calling. It has been spectacular. A lot of terrible times, but a lot of great times. Even with the bad times, it's still good. It's the greatest job on earth."

Joel operates "in the flow." His strength comes from within, through his marriage, through his love of service to his community, and through the firefighter-family culture.

Setting the Context

Most people have optimal experiences while doing what they love most, when time seems to slow or even stand still, and the right decisions come easily. During such episodes, everything feels like it is coming together as it should.[1] There is a heightened awareness around making the right choices, and the impact those choices will have on others and the environment. It feels good to operate in flow.

How might you consciously choose to live your life in this flow state on a regular basis? And how might organizations facilitate flow experiences for their employees, thereby aligning talents with organizational mission, accelerating innovation, fostering a culture of safety, and by extension, increasing personal, organizational, and communal well-being?

Studies by researchers of flow, such as Mihaly Csikszentmihalyi, Martin Seligman, and others, show that the more experience and training a person has in a given area or task, the more flow experiences that person will have. My own doctoral research confirmed this assessment. I looked at the flow experiences of firefighters. I wanted to know if being in a flow state facilitated decision making. The answer is "Yes," if the firefighter has enough training and experience.[2]

One of the participants in my study was David Rhodes. Rhodes is a Battalion Chief in the City of Atlanta, Georgia, Fire Rescue Department. Chief Rhodes also heads up an extreme experiential training program for structural firefighters in the Georgia Fire Service called Georgia Smoke Diver (GSD). GSD is to the fire service what the Navy Seals program is to the Navy.

After I finished my dissertation, Rhodes invited me to observe a GSD training. What started out as a simple observation has turned into a full-blown ethnography of this group of

---

[1] Csikszentmihalyi, 1993; Seligman, 2002

[2] Glick-Smith, 2011

firefighters. The GSD training program and its organization offer a model for flow-based leadership.

It's a VUCA World

We are living and working in a world full of wicked problems. That is, problems that are so intertwined, it is perilous to try to fix an individual aspect for fear it will have a negative domino effect on all the connections within the issue's domain, and beyond. In addition, events tend to be emergent. Before we have time to make sense of what is going on around us, the entire scene has changed in a way that requires new thinking and new solutions. Over the last 25 years, there have been many studies on how to lead and manage this volatile, uncertain, complex, and ambiguous (VUCA) world of ours.

The military coined the VUCA acronym following the end of the Cold War, but *vuca* is also the Zulu word for "to wake up." Given the emphasis on situational awareness and critical decision making in the uniformed professions, VUCA has a double meaning. These professions have been operating in a VUCA world since their inception.

The goal of flow-based leadership isn't to avoid conflict, or to always have positive outcomes. This just isn't possible in a VUCA world. The goal of flow-based leadership is to establish and maintain an organization that promotes the well-being of individuals involved in the organization, as well as the customers or community in which they serve. When people can trust the organization to keep their best interests at heart, they will be more forgiving when things don't go as planned. There will always be factions who disagree based on their own world view, but if the organization consistently demonstrates and communicates its intentions as honorable and true, those who disagree can still respect the decisions made.

VUCA has become a global issue—not just event-driven—that requires adaptive approaches and strong leadership that is situationally aware and able to develop and communicate a vision, impart understanding and clarity, and facilitate adaptability. This is known in the literature as VUCA-Prime.

Required Cultural Challenges

The culture of the fire service and other similarly structured, uniformed professions is unique in that its members exhibit a sense of duty and allegiance that doesn't often exist in other careers. The resulting culture is integral to the delivery of services to the community. It defines not only how they work with the public, but how they interact with each other on each shift, at their station with other shifts, and with their department in general.[3]

There is a level of camaraderie that has evolved over time due to the very nature of the way the job is structured. Firefighters speak of their shift-mates as family, and their fire station as their house. Everyone is responsible for readiness through house maintenance, equipment maintenance, personal health and wellness, and mental capacity. There is a commitment to group learning through training. Emergency responses also result in group learning during the debriefings following incidents. The culture matures and familial bonds are strengthened during downtime and the informal activities of living, such as meal time, storytelling, and leisure activities.

---

[3] International Association of Fire Chiefs and U.S. Fire Administration, 2015

Chris Wessels, an Assistant Chief with City of Atlanta, Georgia, Fire Rescue Department, told me a story about his traveling to a factory that produced fire apparatus in order to investigate the purchase of a rig for his department. He noticed that at quitting time, the workers at that factory ran out of the building like ants out of a disturbed anthill. He said this just doesn't happen at fire stations; people stand around drinking coffee and talking to the incoming shift. In fact, he said, this is even more prominent in the volunteer departments, where they often keep the equipment and the station house scrubbed and in working order even more meticulously than in paid departments. This seems counterintuitive to the idea that people are motivated solely by monetary compensation.

However, there is a downside to this closeness and family orientation. Sometimes it can work against beneficial change, either through the introduction of new ways of doing things or improving processes based on experiences.

On June 18, 2007, the Charleston, South Carolina, Fire Department lost nine firefighters in the line of duty. Only one of the nine called a Mayday, which is a communication that a firefighter makes when he or she is in a life-threatening situation. That firefighter had received training from outside the Charleston Fire Department. Traditions in the Charleston Fire Department perpetuated the thinking that to call a Mayday was somehow unmanly or less brave. Therefore, there were eight firefighters, indoctrinated in the Charleston culture, who did not call a Mayday. This is a perfect example of how hanging onto tradition, even when safety is compromised, can be dangerous.

In April, 2015, the International Association of Fire Chiefs and the U.S. Fire Administration published the "National Safety

Culture Change Initiative" report. This document makes the case for moving the emergency and fire service "toward a safety culture." Deeply ingrained traditions can impact the ability to change. Efforts to implement new ways of doing things are perceived as "challenges to fundamental beliefs."

When I tell people who are not in the fire service that I'm researching decision making in the fire service, the conversation often turns toward the perceived risk-taking behaviors of firefighters. However, risk-taking behaviors "have been shown to be an organizational problem and not one that lies solely with firefighters' behaviors."[4] This points directly to leadership. It is the responsibility of leaders to set the example and communicate the vision of a culture of safety. While the declaration "Everyone goes home!" is a worthy mantra, organizations need to put in place the tools, procedures, and training that facilitate the changes in culture to make this a reality every day.

Building an effective culture requires diligence, commitment, a focus on safety, a servant-leadership orientation, knowledge management, a sense of honor and duty to doing what is right and true, a willingness to accept risk, thoughtful decision making, and mindful communication. While there is no one magic formula for guaranteeing that an organization will be flow-based and run smoothly, the components described in this book, applied consistently and with integrity, will help you and your organization move with purpose and intent to be successful. Briefly, these components are:

1.   Lead by example.

---

[4] International Association of Fire Chiefs and U.S. Fire Administration, 2015

2. Foster a communicative culture by regularly articulating your vision to instill a sense of purpose.
3. Establish and maintain an infrastructure that supports the work of the organization.
4. Bind the group and cultivate trust with ritual, storytelling, laughter, and collaboration.
5. Honor individual creativity.
6. Use positive motivation techniques.
7. Learn what gives people joy, offer training to enhance their strengths, and give them the opportunities to work in that space.

Who This Book Is For

This book is directed at those people who lead and work in the world of public safety, where situations are emergent and decisions have to be made quickly and correctly. Whether you fight fire, respond to medical emergencies, manage the conflict of a domestic dispute, repair track for a major metropolitan transit system, care for a gunshot victim in an emergency room, defend the United States on foreign shores, or make sure that planes do not have mid-air collisions, my hope is that the information presented here will inspire you to see your organization and your personal commitment to "the job" in a new light.

The people who commit their lives to public service often think of their job as a calling, but it is human nature to be comfortable in our chosen routines. As you read this book, I invite you to do a 360 size-up on how you think of the job and of your life. Just as you size up an incident, mentally walk around to the Charlie side, that is, to the side that you can't normally see, and take a look at your world from a different angle.

This book may make you feel off balance. Keep in mind, we only grow when we are a bit off balance. On the other hand, it might validate everything you already believe. In either case, I hope that it will enrich your thinking about the work you do, and have the effect of enhancing your sense of pride about your chosen profession. Your work is critical to society at its base level, but you also serve as exemplars for society on what it means to do honorable, compassionate work in service to others.

What This Book Is About

This book provides a roadmap—a manifesto—for individuals and public service organizations who want to:

- Align the organizational mission and purpose with those who do the work of the organization.
- Facilitate flow experiences for themselves and their employees, improving decision making, enhancing situation awareness and critical thinking, accelerating innovation, and increasing personal, organizational, and communal well-being.

Ultimately, this framework gives you the tools to initiate and sustain a culture of safety within your organization.

In the last 20 years, there have been multiple studies in how people make decisions.[5] By definition, being in the flow means that you are making the right decisions within the context of an

[5] Beilock, 2010; Ford, 2010; Gasaway, 2009; Gladwell, 2005, 2008; Goleman, 1998; Kahneman, 2011; Klein, 1999, 2003, 2009; H. L. Thompson, 2010

activity.[6] With the exception of the work of Mihaly Csikszentmihalyi and my own doctoral work, relatively little research has been conducted on how being in a flow state actually facilitates appropriate decision making, or how flow-based leadership can facilitate better decision making within an organization. Likewise, while books on leadership have focused on service, sustainability of organizations, and transformation, until recently, Csikszentmihalyi and Pink were the only ones to have connected leadership to facilitating flow for better organizational outcomes.[7] In addition, in a collaboration with ALEAS Simulations, Inc., which is based in California and Hungary, Csikszentmihalyi is using gaming to teach organizations how to build flow-based environments. The collaboration has also produced an e-book, *The Missing Link Discovered©*, to accompany the game.[8] As people use the game to learn about flow-based leadership, ALEAS is collecting data to further fine-tune the research.

It is my hope that my book adds to this body of knowledge by advocating for the combination of mindful organization development, servant leadership, and experiential training. The organization that operates with purpose and is able to communicate that purpose to its members facilitates alignment between the people doing the work of the organization and the organization's stated goals. However, this must be accompanied by outward focus toward those being served by the organization, standardized processes, a solid infrastructure, and a commitment to training to promote flow-based decision making. I call this flow-based leadership.

---

[6] Csikszentmihalyi, 1988

[7] Csikszentmihalyi, 2003; Pink, 2011

[8] Marer, Buzady, & Vecsey, 2015

How This Book Is Organized

My research has been conducted in the fire service. The examples and stories herein are mostly from this research. However, the concepts I present are applicable to all uniformed services, and can actually extend to other organizations. My hope is that you will glean understanding applicable to your own organization from these fireground lessons, and that this book will motivate you to employ the ideas herein in a strategic way. In many cases, this framework will require a culture change. However, a commitment to change will not only increase the skill and well-being of public service professionals, it will also result in better situational decision making, and hopefully, help reduce the number of accidents and deaths in the line of duty.

Chapter 1 provides a history of the study of flow. It breaks down the components of flow and gives concrete and compelling examples of how being in a flow state facilitates situational awareness and critical thinking, which results in better decision making, especially in critical situations.

Chapter 2 discusses the preconditions, the triggers of flow, and techniques for how to consciously initiate flow. It also addresses those times when flow doesn't happen as expected.

Chapters 3 and 4 further define and illustrate the concepts of flow-based decision making and flow-based leadership, including how individuals and organizations currently think about decision making. These chapters set the stage for shifting our paradigm to begin looking at how to facilitate flow-based decisions, both in our personal lives and in the organizations where we work.

Chapter 5 provides a high-level overview of the Georgia Smoke Diver (GSD) program. The GSD program is an extreme, experiential training program in the fire service focusing on mental, as well as physical aspects, much like military special forces Navy Seals, Army Rangers, or the Green Berets. GSD has been in existence since 1978, and has managed to "evergreen" its leadership purposefully and consistently over the years. GSD serves as a model for the flow-based organizational framework presented in Chapter 6.

Chapter 6 describes the flow-based organizational framework derived from the GSD program, which addresses the question: "How will you integrate these components into your life and organization to facilitate situational awareness, a safety mindset and culture, flow-based decision making, critical thinking, and innovation?"

1 What Flow Is

"The problem of meaning will be resolved as the individual's purpose merges with the universal flow."

—Mihaly Csikszentmihalyi

What, exactly, is flow? Consider an activity you enjoy. You are working toward clear goals and receiving immediate feedback. There are many opportunities for decisive action. Action and awareness merge. You concentrate on the task at hand to the exclusion of all information except that which is necessary to the activity. You experience a sense of control. You are unaware of your own consciousness. Time has no meaning, or it is distorted. For example, it slows down, speeds up, or you experience no awareness of time passing. You do the activity for the sake of the doing.

This feeling is called *flow*.

The term *flow* came out of the rigorous research of Mihaly Csikszentmihalyi, who originally referred to the concept as "optimal experience."[9] Flow is a technical term describing those exceptional moments where time has no meaning and actions feel effortless.[10] Csikszentmihalyi found that when conditions are right, flow can come from any activity, and that everyone experiences flow states occasionally. Flow occurs when you face a clear set of challenging goals that require appropriate responses. Training, experience, and access to feedback in the moment facilitate your decision making and your actions. You experience the feeling of complete and infinite immersion in the activity. Flow does not occur when you are at rest.

Intense flow experiences are rare, but you can increase flow experiences by improving your skills in an activity. Some people refer to these moments of intense flow as "being in the zone," standing out "as the best moments in their lives." You are unaware of conflict or contradictions. As a general rule, people pursue activities that interest or reward them. Therefore, most people can experience flow and are rewarded with the feeling of being fully involved at their highest potential.

However, being in a flow state does not guarantee the appropriate decision, experience, or outcome. Flow is neutral: that is, neither positive nor negative.[11]

> Optimal experience is a form of energy, and energy can be used either to help or to destroy... Energy is power, but power is only a means. The goals to which it is applied can make life either richer or more painful.[12]

---

[9] Csikszentmihalyi, 1988

[10] Csikszentmihalyi, 1993, 1997

[11] Csikszentmihalyi, 1990

[12] *Ibid*

The autotelic nature of flow makes it possible for someone who derives enjoyment from doing harm to others to make terrible decisions while in a flow state. Doing harm to others is an example of misuse of flow energy.

Studies have shown that "many of our social problems are due to a lack of flow in everyday life."[13] The more complex your level of consciousness, the greater the contribution to harmony and happiness in your life and in the world. Complexity of consciousness is a function of knowledge, cognition, feelings, and actions. It involves being aware and in control of your unique potential. It also involves creating synchronization between goals and desires, sensations, and experiences for yourself and for others. Flow enables us to have more fulfilling lives, and to create a better future.[14]

My cousin Eric Gall Glickrieman, an improvisational composer, described the feeling of flow as "riding the wave of action." In these moments, he *knows* that he is being authentic. People who report a high frequency of flow experiences are happier and more satisfied with life in general.[15]

Beginnings of Flow Theory

The field of positive psychology is relatively new—built on the work of Carl Jung, Fritz Perls, and Carl Rogers, among others.[16] However, these early leaders focused on helping mentally nonfunctioning people back to a point of functioning in the world. Positive psychology grew out of the desire of people such

[13] Csikszentmihalyi, 1993

[14] *Ibid*

[15] *Ibid*

[16] Seligman, 2002

as Mihaly Csikszentmihalyi and Martin Seligman to focus on how to make healthy people happier, rather than focusing on the pathologies of unhealthy people and neglecting the positive side of life. Out of this work came the quantification of flow.

During the 1970s, a number of researchers began looking at intrinsic motivation and specifically "the quality of subjective experience."[17] In his initial study, Csikszentmihalyi and some of his students studied 200 people who were very good at what they did. These people included athletes, chess masters, and music composers. The participants were asked to describe activities when these activities were going very well. The study's major contribution was "to identify across the widely diverse activities, a common experience that the respondents felt was *autotelic*, or rewarding in and of itself. Eventually, we came to call this experience *flow*." Since this initial study, which became the basis for the book *Flow: The Psychology of Optimal Experience*, Csikszentmihalyi has studied thousands of people in a variety of activities in the United States and around the world. He developed the experience sampling method (ESM) to quantify the data collected in his studies.

> The ESM uses a pager or a programmable watch to signal people to fill out two pages in a booklet they carry with them. Signals are programmed to go off at random times within two-hour segments of the day, from early morning to 11 p.m. or later. At the signal, the person writes down where she is, what she is doing, what she is thinking about, who she is with, and then rates her state of consciousness at the moment on various numerical scales—how happy she is, how much she is concentrating, how strongly she

---

[17] Allison & Duncan, 1998; Csikszentmihalyi, 1988; Fave & Massimini, 1988; Logan, 1988; Seligman, 2002

is motivated, how high her self-esteem is, and so on.[18]

The quantitative data collected using ESM has enabled researchers to develop an accurate and consistent description of the characteristics of flow.

Characteristics of Flow

There are eight characteristics of flow:

- You have clear goals and are receiving immediate feedback within the activity.
- There are many opportunities for decisive action.
- Awareness and action merge.
- You focus on the task at hand.
- You feel in control of your actions.
- Awareness of self disappears during the task and feels stronger following task completion.
- The concept of time has no meaning.
- The experience is autotelic.

When I conducted my research, I interviewed 16 firefighters: eight men and eight women who had at least seven years of experience in the fire service. After explaining the definition of flow, each individual firefighter lit up in recognition of the concept. He or she may have referred to the flow state as something else (for example, "bringing my A-game" or "being in the zone"), but he or she knew the feeling to which I was referring. This section describes the characteristics of flow in the context of this research, and relates some of the representative stories for each characteristic.

---

[18] Csikszentmihalyi, 1997

Clear Goals and Feedback

When you are in a flow state, you are working toward clear goals and are receiving feedback in the moment. Clear goals enable planning. The number one priority during any critical incident is safety, both for the firefighters and the public. Saving buildings and minimizing property loss is secondary to saving lives. Planning is done on the spot and within the context of these goals.

Retired Captain Marguerite Gay Jones (Sacramento, California Fire Department) related the following story about a "vehicle vs. pedestrian" call. Jones talked about being aware of and having to act on concurrent, nonlinear goals:

> "It was a really sad situation. An elderly gentleman was pulling into or out of his driveway and ran over his adult daughter. It was terrible. The woman was under the car's tire. She was unconscious. I don't know if she had expired at that point, but we treated her like a live patient. My crew followed me to take a look... We looked at each other, and one of my firefighters said, 'Let's just lift the car.' I said, 'Yeah! Let's do it.' There were six of us. In two seconds, we picked up the car. The medics did a longitudinal pull to get the lady out. She was loaded into the ambulance and on the way to the hospital in a couple of minutes.

> "My crew and I knew we needed to get the woman out from under the car, get her lowered and gone, and get some help for the dad and the family, whoever might have been there. All of that was right there in front of me. I could see those two or three things I had to do. It happens a lot, where I take one look and I have my little

priority list of what I have to do in the blink of an eye."

Feedback in the moment facilitates immediate adjustment to your decision making. Feedback can come from anywhere, whether it is a person giving feedback or changing circumstances as a result of the current activity.

Opportunities for Decisive Action

Opportunities for acting decisively come from challenging activities that require skill, which are matched by how well a person believes he or she is suited for the challenge. Entering a flow state or "bringing your A-game" is "what is needed on very critical situations, where decisions must be made in rapid succession and concurrently," according to Plymouth, Minnesota, Fire Chief Richard Kline. "In our business, when you are on your game, that's when things flow."

> "When I have that flow going, I am able to recognize that very quickly and say, 'Hey, I don't have the people en route or on the scene to be able to accomplish my goals.' I need to compensate for that and change my goals to account for the lack of staffing."

Lieutenant Kevin Wells validated this thinking when he told me about being dispatched to a fire one night. As his team traveled to the fire, he was preparing and setting up.

> "I was starting to get everything lined up. As we went down the road, all of a sudden, the rookie behind me yelled in the headsets, 'The house behind us is on fire!' Now, it wasn't the [house] that was dispatched to us. It just happened to be on the street we were going into the neighborhood. I said, 'Seriously?' I didn't trust

what he thought he saw. He was sitting backwards. I was sitting forwards, so I didn't see it. He saw it because it was on the B side of the house. A is the front. B is the side. So, from his point of view, it was right there. But from my point of view, I didn't see it. He said, 'I swear! I swear!'

"I said, 'Okay.' I listened to the radio, and it wasn't there. I'm worried. It would be embarrassing if I called in another fire and it wasn't a fire."

Because Wells' arrival to the fire to which his squad was originally dispatched was already covered by other firefighters, he felt comfortable in diverging from his original mission. However,

"Everything I prepared for the first fire was no longer valid. I had to prepare in a flash, and do the radio traffic to let everyone know I had a fire. We really work hard to have a relaxed radio traffic... I took command of the situation and tried to direct guys with what I needed done... [At one point,] I told one truck I needed him to do something. I turned around and they were gone. They went to the other fire. It was all on the fly.

"The flow starts as soon as the call's banged out. As soon as that alarm drops, that flow starts. You start getting in the zone, preparing yourself, what you are going to need, how you are going to do it, getting the work to the guys in trouble, what you are going to do. Then, all of a sudden, for it to be totally blown up and technically almost rebuilt, which you almost never do to a certain point... You still rely on your training. I need to get that done, but it's not as linear as a normal call. I need a fire truck

set up. I need a search set up. I need that set up.
Now, all of a sudden, I'm there and I need to do
a complete size-up."

Awareness and Action Merge

Being aware in the moment is the act of "presencing."
Awareness, especially comprehensive situational awareness, is
necessary to enable you to guide the dynamics in a situation. It
has to happen at multiple levels. You have to be aware of
internal feelings and your physical well-being, the presence of
others in the environment, and the environment itself. There is
no sequential cause-and-effect dynamic between awareness and
action. They are one and the same.

Battalion Chief Paige Colwell (Forsyth County, Georgia Fire
Department), recalled deciding when and where to intubate a
woman who was trapped in her car, after spending 20 minutes
talking to her as the other firefighters cut the car away to free
her. Colwell knew that she couldn't make two or three attempts
to do what she needed to do. "It had to happen, and it had to
happen *now*."

When I asked, "As you stayed with the woman when they were
cutting her out of the car, did you plan your strategy for what
you were going to do when they cut her free?" Colwell surprised
me by saying, "No. It doesn't happen like that. All of those
moments…are not usually pre-thought… It happens in
situations where I have one shot, or when something
desperately has to happen right now." The instant the woman
was free, Colwell acted and was able to intubate the woman
before the other responders removed her from the car. Colwell
knew what to do based on a variety of factors that were familiar
to her. Had the woman been in a different position, non-

responsive, or the weather conditions were different, Colwell may have taken a different approach. But in that moment, her awareness and actions were one.

Cherokee Firefighter Angela Waagen posted this story on social media in January 2016:

> "Despite fifteen years in public safety, it's still terrifying to look up and see adults frantically trying to help a choking fifteen-month-old in a restaurant. *I don't remember walking over* [emphasis added], but suddenly I heard myself say 'I'm a paramedic. Is he choking?' Of course he was choking, he was beet red and turning purple. Thank you, God, that was resolved as easily as it was! Never been so happy to be puked on."

Those who live their lives in service to others and who have the proper training and experience enter flow effortlessly. Waagen didn't take the time to trigger her flow state. Awareness (recognition of a familiar pattern, facilitated through training and experience) and action ("I don't remember walking over") happened at the exact same moment.

Focus on the Task at Hand

When you focus on the task at hand, concerns outside the scope of the flow activity fall away. All the while, you must remain aware of surroundings and the dynamics of the situation, and continue to solicit feedback to make appropriate decisions.

Deputy Chief Ben Barksdale's (Prince George County, Maryland, Fire Department) task on September 11, 2001, was to ventilate the roof of the Pentagon next to where the plane crashed. One of his men was overcome with exhaustion.

"We were focused on getting the task done. I was so in the flow, that, when he collapsed, it didn't take me out of it. I was still able to direct companies to do what I thought we needed to do as far as hooking and trying to get into the roof's structure. I made sure he was going to be okay, but I didn't divert all my focus to him."

Often, the firefighter focuses so much on the task at hand that he or she doesn't remember extraneous information unrelated to the task. For example, Barksdale also spoke about the effort to continue the rescue effort and clean up at the Pentagon.

"We were there for fourteen days. We worked with guys from the USAR [Unit Search and Rescue] teams from Memphis and Arizona. Later in the year, when I was traveling and happened to run into them, they said, 'Yeah, I saw you at the Pentagon.' I didn't remember. They said, 'Yeah, we could tell. All you guys were just like machines. We could tell you were doing the work, but you weren't processing the conversations that had nothing to do with the work.'"

Joel Kanasky told a story about how he was so focused on a task that he didn't even recognize the people involved with him in the incident:

"[Some] events are pretty dramatic. You don't even realize you are even into it. [In the Jerome Avenue incident in the Bronx,] we lost two firemen and the building collapsed. One of the guys that I dug out and put in the Stokes basket and got out of the building was a dear friend for around 18 years. I didn't know it was him until the next day. I never knew it. I had no idea.

"Sometimes, when I'm playing the game, I don't pay attention to the things around me, except for the game. When the captain and I crawled to him, he was buried from the waist down. He kept telling me over and over his leg was on fire. We kept telling him, 'We're going to get you out.' We kept digging, digging, digging. We got him out, got him in the Stokes basket, sent him on his way, and I never realized it was my dear friend.

"He lived, but he's off the job because he was burned so badly. I never had a clue it was him. It was funny because I never talked to him about it. I knew it was him afterwards. He went to the hospital. I visited him at the burn center. But I never talked about the job with him.

"[Two years later], we were in Alexandria doing a seminar. He was giving a lecture, and I was giving another. In one of the lectures, at the end, he talked about this collapse and how it changed his life because of being trapped for that moment. He kept talking about this guy who kept yelling at him to shut up and who put the webbing underneath him. He said he never knew who it was. But it was actually me who was yelling at him to shut up, and who put the webbing underneath him. He didn't know.

"He hadn't tuned into me at all. It was totally amazing. There was smoke there, but it wasn't anything you couldn't see through... It was amazing that two years had passed before we actually had a beer over it and talked about it."

Confidence: The Feeling of Being in Control

Flow experiences give you the sense that you are in control, and not worried about losing control. The ability to feel a sense of control is facilitated by training and preparation. More accurately, according to Csikszentmihalyi, flow enables feelings of "the possibility of control...what people enjoy is not the sense of being in control, but the sense of exercising control in difficult situations." The byproduct of feeling a sense of control is confidence.

A number of firefighters talked about the aspect of confidence and the sense of control within the context of flow. Paige Colwell tempered her comments about confidence by saying she knows not to ever be overconfident about anything.

> "As soon as you think you are good at something, something will happen to show you that you are not God. You might be good at something, but there are going to be situations where the best you can do is not going to happen, like a pulmonary embolism... It doesn't matter what I do. It's going to end up that way, even with your best efforts. You can't get everything right; there's nothing you can do."

I asked Ben Barksdale how he and his crew were able to work at the Pentagon on 9/11 for 36 hours straight. At first he said, "Adrenaline," but he followed with:

> "How you are trained. If a person is confident in how they have been trained and what they have been trained on, and as long as they are successful in carrying out the mission, everything just moves along. I think it is when things don't go well, if you are not able to complete a lot of objectives or whatever the assignments are, then you start reflecting on the negative. You get frustrated and that is where you are not effective, so there is no flow."

While confidence is not directly named as one of the characteristics of flow, it fits with having "a sense of potential control." This is illustrated in a story told by retired Fire Chief Richard Gasaway, Ph.D., [19] (Roseville, Minnesota, Fire Department). He successfully responded to a situation, his first really big incident, when he had no prior experience. He was the first to arrive, and saw a "big fire in a big building." He said he had one of two choices: "One was to freak out, or the other one was to get into the zone and do what I had been taught to do." He was aware of his feelings in the situation, and consciously calmed himself down. All of his communications were calm and direct. He validated this when he listened to the tapes following the incident. His experience with this fire gave him confidence in later incidents.

> "This was the biggest fire of my career, and I can't even describe how I knew what to do, but I did. It flowed like I was an orchestra leader leading an orchestra... I was 'game on' and just knew what to do, what to have other people do, and deal with all the little problems that were coming along the way. It just seemed like I was unshakable... I had a comfort level with commanding, but I didn't have a comfort level of commanding an incident of that size... That particular incident influenced me in later incidents... It gave me a confidence that, when I'm under that kind of stress, instead of freaking out, I will calm down... I think that incident helped to build my confidence that there is a...zone state that I can get into that will help me through a large-scale incident...everything I'm doing feels right... When you are doing it and you are doing it well, and it feels good and you are in the zone, confidence seems to be a logical byproduct of that state of being."

---

[19] http://www.samatters.com/ and http://www.richgasaway.com/

The success he had commanding that incident, coupled with his training and previous experience, gave him confidence that if he could command an incident of that size, he could "handle just about anything."

Many firefighters mentioned feeling good after an incident, no matter what the outcome. This raised their confidence level and the sense of being able to be in control during an incident. Kevin Wells told me about an incident he was involved in as a volunteer in a rural department with limited resources.

> "We had a fire one time that was perfect, where another guy and I went in. We fought fire. The truck showed up. They did the truck work. Everybody did their own little job, like you would in a normal department. Everyone came out and did cleanup and got out of there. Usually, here, you have to do the job of overhaul and then you do your own cleanup. When you are done with a fire here, you are just worn out, because you have to do your own work... We had that fire that was just perfect. That was kind of nice."

I loved how Battalion Chief Jodi Gabelmann (Cobb County, Georgia Fire Department and Georgia Smoke Diver #481) told the story about a similar incident that she called "perfect."

> "It was rippin'! We got there and everybody [occupants] was accounted for. It was like a pop-up book, you know, like a kid's book? Those guys were like bangity-bang, and things were done! I mean with just minor snafus, just minor glitches. We rolled up and when we saw smoke and fire, we thought, 'Oh, okay.' Then we saw structural members... People got off the rig and bada bing, bada boom, and it went, "Whoop!" That was like, "Wow!" And this was our first big

incident since I took over that battalion. I was like, "Damn! Y'all were banging! Good deal! Hope they all go like that!" It was pretty awesome."

There is a confidence about "just knowing," about recognizing familiar circumstances, and by extension, feeling a potential for control. Gay Jones recalled the confidence she had when arriving on the scene of a church fire.

"My twenty years of experience kicked in. I recognized that this was a classic church fire. I knew that I was going to have an early collapse, because the church had so much air in the alcove. The whole church was so open. It sounds so simple, but all that came to me at once— check, check, check, check, check. I knew the church was a goner, but nobody got hurt."

Confidence also seems to be a function of knowing what you do well. For example, David Rhodes was involved in a multiday incident when a large Atlanta hospital had lost its water supply. Rhodes was confident in the knowledge his team brought to the situation.

"I knew nothing about running a hospital... What we are good at is breaking the problems down into manageable pieces and knowing what to call them. We may not know exactly how to accomplish what needs to be done, but we know how to identify who in the organization would probably be the key person.

"We set up the command structure and got rid of two-thirds of the people that were there, keeping just the key folks. We developed a really quick plan. In a fire department we have operations, which would be somebody who was familiar with all the tactics and strategies that we use to fight fire. Our plan was to determine how to keep the hospital running and how we would evacuate the hospital and transfer twelve hundred patients, if it came to that."

Rhodes' team developed a plan for hooking up a fire engine to a fire hydrant, running a fire hose up through the parking deck, and supplying water to the chillers needed to keep the hospital running. "That's what we do. We move water." The city water department held a briefing about how they were going to fix the water problem. They explained that they were going to have to shut 17 valves in the city blocks surrounding the hospital. They insisted that when they shut down these valves, there would still be water available to the firefighters and the hospital. Rhodes did not have any confidence in the water department's statements.

> "Without saying a word to them, I made a little note to create a backup plan for that water. I wasn't confident that they really knew what shutting seventeen valves was going to do. As soon as we left, I called our mutual aid group in Georgia (GMAG), which is a shared resource throughout the state. I asked them if they could send us a water tanker strike team, which consists of five tankers that hold two to three thousand gallons apiece. All our engines only hold five hundred gallons. In the rural areas, tanker operations are how they fight fire. We don't do that in [our metropolitan area]. We don't shuttle water. We hook up to a hydrant and do our thing.

> "I didn't need just the trucks, because our folks would have to learn how to use them. What I needed was expertise in how to move a lot of water, just like we would on a fire. They sent in a five-tanker strike team from multiple counties.

We designed a route so that everybody was going in a circle and wouldn't need to back up. The tankers were constantly going. We got all the drop tanks and other equipment that we needed. We set it up so that if our hydrant went dry and the engine couldn't get water, we could just drop a suction hose into a tank and these trucks could keep filling up.

"We staged our trucks and the tankers. The water department didn't wait for us to begin work on the water valves. They were in the process of shutting down. They got to around valve fifteen, and we lost all water in the entire area. The only thing that kept the hospital functioning was that we had put those tanker shuttles in place. They ran for twelve to sixteen hours, just shuttling water constantly, keeping those chillers going. It wasn't a ton of water per minute, when you look at the travel time. I think we had to maintain about two hundred fifty gallons per minute into the chiller, and your drop tanks would hold about fifteen hundred gallons. But nobody had to drive like mad. It was a *system* [emphasis added]."

People in the hospital asked, "How did you come up with that idea?" Rhodes explained that it was because of experience with things failing in the past.

"It came from the experience of knowing, when you are in that position, you cannot one hundred percent rely on the information you get. You have to use your gut instinct from your experience, so that you can recover when something happens."

Losing Sense of Self

In a flow state, you experience transcendence beyond your ego boundaries. There is a sense of growth, and of being part of some greater entity. This leaves more psychic energy to concentrate on what needs to be done.

This was evident in every story told. This manifested as a change in tense and voice in the story the firefighter was telling. He or she began in first or third person, past tense, but ended in second person, present tense. This was very apparent in those direct and intimate interactions with victims.

In a subsequent discussion about September 11, 2001, Ben Barksdale spoke about his fire service brothers at the World Trade Center and their selfless sacrifice.

> "I think back to what was going on up in New York up in the Trade Center, and…firefighters make choices every day… I get a little emotional, but, in my mind, those guys KNEW that they were not going to make it out. It was a matter of how many people can we save? I think Captain Hadden's wife said it best: 'He made a choice that day.' He was captain of Rescue 1 and was killed. He made a choice that day— that he was willing to give his life that day and sacrificed his family, but that's the choice that he made. He knew he wasn't coming out of there."

Rich Gasaway observed the loss of self-consciousness while in a flow state:

> "Maybe part of the thing about being in the zone is that, in the moment, you don't realize that you are in the zone… I'd like to think that somewhere along the way, I'm consciously doing

it, but I think that the result of it is probably
not conscious. I don't think that I have the
ability to consciously tap into memory stores
that are dormant when I'm not under stress. It's
the incident that taps me into areas that I don't
think that I can consciously access. I might be
able to if I concentrated very hard, but I would
say that it is more likely it's not conscious."

Helen Graham, Deputy Fire Staff Officer (equivalent to deputy
chief) and Forest Aviation Officer for Tonto National Forest in
Arizona, spoke of the Mudd fire, a wildland fire. A couple of
firefighters from Helen's agency (the Bureau of Land
Management) were involved in an entrapment burnover while
fighting the Mudd fire. At the time of the incident, Graham was
on her way to another fire, in another state. Her national
operations lead called her to be part of the investigation team
for the Mudd fire.

"Knowing that at least one of my engines was
on the fire, I said, 'Yeah, you know one of my
engines is on the fire?' He said, 'That's why I'm
asking. Are you going to be too close to this?' I
said, 'No, I can separate myself. I can be on the
team and not be personally involved.'"

The firefighters who were caught in this fire were not treated
appropriately by the local rural hospital. They were seen in the
emergency room and released to a hotel. It turns out that their
burns were extensive, but because of the nature of flash burns,
this wasn't immediately apparent to the clinical staff. They
were not used to seeing these types of burns.

The Mudd fire became the impetus for drastic changes in how
wildland fire burn victims were managed thereafter. Graham's
conscious choice to be involved in the investigation led her to
believe "there should be a better way to define when our folks

need to go to a burn unit." She began to collaborate on research with a nurse at the Arizona Burn Center at Maricopa County Hospital to identify what is common in burns that happen in a wildland setting, most of which get treated in a rural setting by health care personnel not familiar with these types of burns. She used this research to develop and implement a policy that was ultimately adopted nationally. In other words, she was able to separate herself from being personally involved to affect change in the form of national policy, which has helped prevent life altering injuries from becoming aggravated or disabling from the lack of appropriate care. Firefighters now feel empowered to insist on being sent to a burn unit for treatment when burned in a wildland fire. Graham said, "We weren't going to have it happen again. Putting that policy in place empowered the local folks to take the actions that they needed to take."

There were two stories in my doctoral study that involved the resuscitation of an infant when the firefighter/EMS technician took selfless action. Gay Jones was called out because of a nonresponsive baby. She had checked the suction unit that morning—but when she got to the scene, it didn't work. She used the tubing ordinarily used for delivering oxygen as a big, long straw.

> "I sucked out the mucus and vomit—the stuff that was in the baby's throat—to clear the airway. I did that all right away, while I was thinking about doing mouth-to-mouth. Once I cleared the airway, I went ahead and did mouth-to-mouth, even though I knew that was not the normal protocol."

Captain Anne Marsh (Arlington, Virginia Fire Department) was involved in a similar incident. She also felt she was doing the right thing, but "at great, great personal cost." She and the fire chief were on their way to a conference when they heard a call go out for a "trouble-breathing infant." They were only a block away. Marsh thought that she might be able to do something to save the infant, since they were so close.

> "It turned out to be a cardiac arrest of an infant. The fire chief is not an EMT... I'm a medic. That's what I do. I went in.
>
> "The babysitter was trying to do rescue breathing on a three-month-old infant. I took over and was doing mouth-to-mouth and chest compressions on the infant. I tried to clear the airway. I had no equipment; it was just me. I was suctioning the baby's mouth and nose with my mouth. The baby had just been fed. The mother had expressed breast milk for the baby. The mother was not there. It was being fed through a bottle with the breast milk in it. I breast-fed both my children and could taste that sweet taste of the breast milk on this poor, little dead baby, who was not resuscitated. There was no positive outcome on this one... I never got over that. Never."

Firefighters make no judgments about the "other." What sets firefighters apart is their compassion for other people.[20] The firefighter helps without prejudice or attribution. There are no labels placed on the people (or animals) in jeopardy. Firefighters are called to save lives. This calling serves as the link among them.[21] Chief Frank Walsh (New Jersey) said, "The greatest uniform that a man can wear is that of a fireman. It is greater than even the Army or the Navy. Theirs reminds us of the loss

[20] Smith, 1988
[21] Taylor & Wolin, 2002

of human life, whereas that of the fireman is dedicated to its saving."[22]

Retired District Chief Michael McNamee (Worcester, Massachusetts Fire Department) told me about the aftermath of the incident he was involved in when his department lost six firefighters.

> "Our chief was actually questioned back then, 'Why did your men go in there looking for homeless people?' In a very calm and dignified manner, [the chief] responded: 'We don't do a sociological analysis before we go into a situation.'
>
> "A situation calls for a certain action. That's what we are trained to do. That's what we do. That's who we are. That's why we do it. We don't care if you're rich. We don't care if you're poor. We don't care color. We don't care religion. If you need us, that's what we do for a living. In our job, if you are in it long enough, for most people, it becomes a large part of who you are, even outside the job."

This particular event was enormous and had far reaching implications. I have yet to talk to a firefighter who is not familiar with the Worcester fire in December 1999. McNamee was involved as an incident commander on this incident, and was the one who ultimately made the decision to change the mission from rescue to recovery, and not send in anymore firefighters to look for the ones who were lost. He was also the one the chief asked to do the press briefing after the fire was extinguished, three days later. When he asked the chief how he should handle the press, the chief told him, "Tell them what

---

[22] Granito, 2003

happened." McNamee was relieved that the department was going to be open about what happened.

> "There is a tendency to go into bunker mode. A lot of departments try to hide what happened. We didn't do anything wrong that night. We fought that fire the way we fought a thousand others, and the building just beat us... We were an open book right from the beginning. This attitude really helped us get through this. Here's what happened. Here's how it went down. Honesty is the best policy."

This particular department began to give seminars all over the country as a result of this incident.

Loss of self-consciousness includes the willingness to ask for help and expertise outside one's own sphere of knowledge. In the midst of trying to shore up a collapsed parking garage, David Rhodes realized that he needed engineering expertise. He brought in three engineers to assess the situation. "We asked them to work together to figure out, based on each one of their personal areas of expertise, what would be best."

Temporal Distortion

Time morphs when you are in a flow state. During my doctoral research, some firefighters told me that time sped up during critical incidents; others said it slowed down. Several said that they had no concept of time.

Paige Colwell gave one of the most descriptive accounts of an altered sense of time. When she arrived on the scene of a house fire, a woman was screaming in the driveway. She knew that this meant there was a child inside. Colwell grabbed the hose and waited for it to charge (i.e., fill with water). She could still hear the woman screaming in the driveway.

> "I remember everything slowing for me. It was like I took in everything at once. It was like watching a hummingbird's wings slow to where you could see the individual beats. It was an instant. I know it was just an instant that I dropped the hose line and went in."

She made her way down the hallway. There was so much smoke, she was crawling and feeling her way. The woman in the driveway had told her where her "baby" was. Her baby turned out to be a 5-foot, 8-inch, 135-pound, 33-year-old man.

> "I came down on his chest, and, when I pushed down, he breathed out. I heard him. Right at that point—and that was another moment that just slowed for me—just like hummingbird's wings—the window to the bedroom was broken by the guys from the outside, because I remember covering him and screaming, 'I've got him in here!' I reached around; I sat him up. I got around behind him and picked him up. I put my arms underneath him and wrapped around his chest and started to drag him to the window... [When the glass broke,] I just remember throwing myself over the victim. It was almost like I could have picked out individual pieces of glass breaking."

Jodi Gabelmann was involved in another incident when a woman was standing in the driveway screaming. Gabelmann consciously chose to alter time.

> "The first thing I saw when I rolled up was a naked woman howling like a Beowulf, and I knew exactly what that meant. That was the mother. I had to fast-forward past that... This

was all like a film in my head, going a hundred miles an hour. Yet it was so slow, because it was real time and not fast-forward time that all these things were coming together."

Gabelmann also told a personal story about her mother's illness; she was the primary caregiver. She called this her "slow story." Being a firefighter, she was used to evaluating a situation and responding quickly and efficiently. Her mother's illness forced her to be more focused. That experience "felt slow, because I had to focus so much."

Experiencing an altered sense of time is not always desirable, especially as an incident commander. Rich Gasaway gave the following example.

> "On occasion, I have experienced this slowing down of time, where I have a slow-motion sensation, which for me can be good or bad. For example, in this slow-motion state, I'm watching firefighters perform their duties. It appears to me that they are doing their work in slow motion, which can lead to frustration for me. I'm looking at them and saying they should be working faster.

> "As things slow down, for me, everything slows down, including the motion of the firefighters pulling the hose line and putting on their gear. That all goes into a slow-motion state. While I know that it has only taken them a minute to pull that hose line and get it charged and ready to go in the front door, it seems like three or four minutes have gone by because of the way the incident scene and the performance of the firefighters appear to have slowed down. You would find many fireground commanders saying that they sense that things should be going faster than they are.

"The temporal distortion—the slowing down of the time— has also given me the sensation that I have more time to think things through. As things tend to go into a slower state, it doesn't mean I'm thinking slower; it's like I'm buying time. Maybe that's part of being in the zone, as being in this state where I am able to process things. My mind's going fast, but what I'm seeing through my eyes appears to be slowed down. As a commander on an incident, this all just happens."

Gay Jones related how she felt as she arrived on the scene of a church fire.

"When I arrived, I noticed that it was the classic church fire with the bit V roof. The whole back end was on fire. Time felt like it was in slo-mo. Everything was happening very fast, but it felt like slo-mo."

When it came time to make the appropriate decisions on what to do in this situation, she said, "It sounds so simple, but all that came to me at once…"

Mike McNamee had this to say about the sense of time:

"Time is funny in emergency situations. It compresses and expands in very weird ways. If you had asked me how long we'd been searching [for lost firefighters in the Worcester Cold Storage Warehouse fire], I would have said about twenty minutes. Turned out, it was actually an hour and ten minutes. And I never would have guessed that."

Autotelic Experience

Autotelic refers to the idea that one acts for the sake of doing. The flow experience is ultimately satisfying and enjoyable. One is fully immersed in the activity.

Multiple participants in my study mentioned that firefighters are adrenaline junkies, because they love the excitement and challenge of what they do. They love the sense of belonging. As Mike McNamee reflected on his 37 years in the fire service, he said, "For the most part, firefighters are very family oriented, have a tremendous work ethic, and we share an addiction. We are adrenaline junkies... I loved my career. I would do it again in a heartbeat."

While adrenaline may be how they justified their addiction to firefighting, all of the firefighters interviewed spoke of firefighting as a calling. Joel Kanasky told me:

> "It was always a desire and a love... It's such a rewarding thing, teaching kids about what we do. All of that goes hand in hand. That is what keeps me going."

Kanasky reflected about how he and another firefighter (Thor) were able to save themselves in the World Trade Center.

> "I have talked with Thor probably every week for the last nine years, but it was just about keeping my head and making that move. Whether you are in the back of a flat and trying to crawl past the fire or whatever—just making that move without thinking—you just do what you've got to do... You don't think about anything you're doing. You just work."

Gay Jones told the story about being on a call that involved securing an area where there was a downed power line. It was late at night. They were going to be there until morning, when the utility crew could get there. The captain had fallen asleep in the back of the truck. Jones heard the battalion chief come on the radio and tell them to put some cones out and come on in for shift change. Without hesitation she picked up the mike and said, "Negative, Chief."

> Gay Jones continues: "I told him, 'We have a live wire down. We have school kids. We have morning commute. SMUD's still not here. We can't leave.' I remember hearing his frustration on the air. That was a big deal for an engineer to say that to a chief. But it all happened in like ten seconds. That was what needed to be done."

Mike McNamee commented on his decision to turn a rescue effort to a recovery effort in the face of losing six firefighters.

> "Sometimes it's what you have to do. That moment was one of the clearest moments of my life... I know I did [everything right that night]. That's one of the reasons I can live with myself. If I had made some bad calls that night, I wouldn't have bounced back. What we did is what we do."

He commented on the dedication of the men in his command. "I could see a lot of fear in the eyes of those dozens of firefighters who were in line waiting to go up, and I gave them their instructions. But they all went."

The concept of "following your gut" was prevalent in some of the firefighters with long-term experience. In talking about how she handled her department's line of duty death, retired Prince William County, Virginia, Fire Chief Mary Beth Michos said, "There was no checklist to go to for all that stuff. We just had to go by our gut and what we felt were the best things to do."

Mike McNamee confirmed that response, saying, "You follow your gut. After you have been around a long time, and for some reason, something's telling you something, you should listen to that."

Denise Pouget (Director of the Jefferson County Emergency Services Agency in Jefferson County, West Virginia) was involved in the rescue of a teenage girl who was badly hurt in a car accident. The other rescuers wanted to leave the girl to focus on another victim, because they thought she was not going to make it. Pouget made the call to pull the girl out. Later, the doctor on the scene told her that the girl was going to make it, but that her spinal cord had been crushed and that she would probably be quadriplegic permanently. Pouget remarked, "It was an awful feeling, but I felt like I did what I had to do. If I had to make the decision again, I would... That sticks out in my mind when you talk about flow and having to make decisions. Time stands still...and you just get into your groove and do what you have to do."

Kevin Wells said, "On every call, you're doing your thing. All the stories kind of run together. They have similarities." Wells had the least amount of experience of all those I interviewed. He had just become a lieutenant at the time of the interview. He commented on the difference in focus as one attains a higher rank.

> "When you are a fireman, you are doing your thing. You worry about you. You worry about your partner, but it's you. As a fireman, I want to go and dig out. If it's burning seventy percent of the building, I want to go in there and 'get me some.' Once you become an officer, it changes the whole scope. Once you become battalion chief and incident commander, you

ask, 'What's my risk analysis here? Is what I'm getting worth these guys?' They might hate me because I'm pulling them all out and going defensive, but as an officer, it changes everything."

Conclusion

The feeling of being in flow is that of being at peace in any activity. It is that feeling of lightness, of moving without effort, of buoyancy: as if flying through the air or floating in water.

In the summer of 2014, I visited the deputy chief of the Brunswick, Georgia, Fire Department, Jerry Allen (Georgia Smoke Diver #399). Jerry owns a crabbing business in the Brunswick/Savanah area. He had invited me to go out on his boat, while he collected crabs from the traps he had set. We were up at 4 a.m. and on the water before the sun was up. The water was like glass; the air was cool. As we moved swiftly through the marshes to where his traps were located, we saw the most beautiful sunrise and flocks of a variety of sea birds.

I watched Jerry's face as he worked. He was in his element. He was at peace; he was at home. This was his flow state. He stayed in that state from low tide to high tide, as he pulled in and emptied crab traps as fast as his helper could sort and store them. He collected close to 1000 pounds of crabs that morning. All of the characteristics of flow existed in this extended moment of time.

Flow can happen at any time. We all strive for these states, consciously or unconsciously. We have goals, whether we actively acknowledge them or not. There are always an infinite number of opportunities to act decisively. As we receive immediate feedback from our decisions, awareness and action become one, enabling focus. When we let ourselves move into that space where we do the activity for its own sake, we move out of self-consciousness and into a feeling of control. There is no sense of time.

The more flow experiences you have, the happier and more satisfied with life you will be. The feeling is contagious. Through example, you show others what flow looks like. This impacts your coworkers, your family, and ultimately, your community. The next chapter discusses the preconditions of flow, and how you can learn to trigger it.

2 Initiating Flow (or Not)

"Creative suspension is very different from 'doing nothing.' It is an active form of watchfulness and assessment in order to take the most effective action as quickly as possible."

—F. David Peat

People often ask me, "How can I trigger flow?" While the answer is unique to each person, there are specific conditions that must be in place for flow to occur. In addition, my flow triggers are different from yours. In first-responder world, there were very specific triggers of flow. While you can prepare yourself thoroughly through training and experience and put yourself in situations where flow might occur, there are also techniques you can use to consciously initiate flow. We will discuss these steps later in this chapter.

In addition, there are times when flow just doesn't happen, even when all the elements of the situation seem to be in alignment. So much about experiencing flow is allowing awareness and action to merge. The best you can do is to prepare relentlessly, put all the components of flow into place, and learn to let go when you step into the situation. My own personal experience has shown me that when I am intently focused on controlling the situation, my ability to let go is compromised. In these situations, flow cannot happen.

Preconditions of Flow

Flow doesn't happen for everyone. There are those who may never experience flow. For example, some schizophrenics do not have the ability to feel pleasure or joy. Because flow has a feel-good component, it is difficult for these people to enter into flow. In addition, people who are excessively self-absorbed and concerned about what others think may be unable to lose themselves in an activity. Because their focus is directed toward excessively worrying about what others are thinking, these people lack the psychic energy necessary to enter a flow experience.[23] Other than these groups, most people have the ability to enter flow states. But what has to be in place for this to happen?

We each choose our own flow activities, based on the meaning we attach to them. Flow occurs at the intersection of the activity's challenge level and our abilities to meet those challenges. In other words, to enter into flow, we have to balance challenges and skill at a high level, while receiving feedback within and about the activity. It isn't easy to transform into flow, but you can improve your ability to do so. All flow activities are transformative. The more flow experiences you have, the more multifaceted you become.

Csikszentmihalyi devotes an entire chapter to the conditions of flow in his book, *Flow: The Psychology of Optimal Experience.* He

---

[23] Csikszentmihalyi, 1990

explains the process of how we move in and out of flow, as shown in Figure 1: flow activities lead to growth and discovery. However, we can't enjoy an activity at the same level for long. Eventually, we get bored. When we reach the level of boredom, we can either transfer our energies to a new, more challenging activity, or we can hone our skills and return to the original activity to try something more challenging. When we look for more challenging activities, we experience anxiety until we reach a level of confidence that throws us back into a flow state—and the process starts again. The following illustration shows how this works.

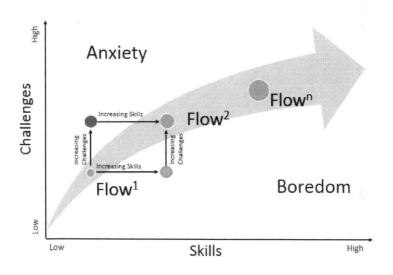

Figure 1: Relationship between Anxiety and Boredom to Flow[24]

I had a wonderful conversation with Captain Richard Bue (GSD #896) of the City of Brunswick Fire Department in Georgia about his quest for knowledge. Like many firefighters, he enjoys challenging himself by attending multiple training courses. After completing the Georgia Smoke Diver program, he

---

[24] Csikszentmihalyi, 2003

decided to go through the Tennessee Smoke Diver program. He had already been through Georgia F.L.A.M.E.S. (Firefighters Laboring and Mastering Essential Skills). Bue is passionate about his work as a firefighter. He simply wants to be the best he can be, on the job and in his life in general. He understands that he can always learn something new in each class. He actively seeks out new opportunities to learn and excel. He explained to me that once he has learned something really well, he strives to challenge himself to go to the next level. In this way, he is always getting better, and enjoying the job and his life more. He is also appreciative of every opportunity to expand his abilities. Bue's proactive learning quest is always preparing him for the next level of flow.

Triggers of Flow

My doctoral research indicated that there are a variety of triggers of flow, including awareness, size-up, and complexity of the situation. There are also physical and psychological readiness ("it feels right") triggers, including stress factors or recognizing that the situation presented as something out of the ordinary (as indicated by words like "weird," "odd," "crazy," etc.). Some firefighters consciously triggered flow and expressed confidence, even though they had never been in a situation like this before. The most common events that triggered flow were (a) a recognition that something was out of the ordinary; (b) a threat to the firefighter's personal or team safety; and (c) child involvement, particularly when the incident began with a woman in the driveway. The preconditions of flow were in place for each of these events. The firefighter felt challenged by something new, different, and, often, unthinkable. Feedback was immediate and ongoing during the event.

Something Out of the Ordinary

Recognition-primed decision making depends on recognizing familiar situations and patterns, and then, based on this recognition, acting according to past experience or training. What throws an individual into a flow state, in which he or she feels challenged, is often something out of the ordinary. In other words, the decision maker recognizes something is a mismatch or anomaly, something outside his or her sphere of experience. The firefighters in this study and in Gary Klein's work talked about using their intuition. However, this was difficult for them to describe. "Firefighters' experience enables them to recognize situations quickly...intuition grows out of experience."[25]

Participants in my study responded to the definitions of flow, creative suspension, and gentle action with stories that immediately came to mind upon hearing the definitions. These stories were most often unusual, which is why they stood out in the participants' minds.

For example, Kevin Wells told the story about a 13-year-old boy, who had been burned over 60 percent of his body. This was not a normal call for this firefighter.

> "I went into his back yard and found this kid burned up. When people burn, it doesn't look bad. You know it's bad from your training, but it doesn't present itself as bad. He was lying on the ground. His skin was peeled off... I was there as an EMT, and I got into this zone and my work, but I was wondering where do I start? I was hoping the medic would show up... You know it's a bad EMS call for the medic to show up. [The medic] told me later he had the same feeling of not knowing where to start on the kid.

[25] Klein, 1998

> We both did what we were trained to do, but
> this was not an everyday medical call that you
> do in your sleep. It's the ones that are way
> outside the box, the ones you don't train on all
> the time, that you try to pull up from memory
> on how to do it right."

The stories the firefighters told were out of the ordinary. There were triggers such as sensory awareness ("the taste of breast milk," "there was a woman screaming in the driveway"). They used words like "something wasn't right," "it was a crazy night," "it was weird," "the building was evil." All of these were indications that the incident or situation was unusual. The firefighters were aware of the differences from both training and their previous experience. The deviation from the expected was the trigger for the flow state.

Threat to Personal Safety

Dr. Joseph McNamara, volunteer firefighter with a suburban fire department in Georgia, was involved in an incident in which fireworks were being set off at a friend's home on the lake during a party. His family was with him. Prior to the fireworks display, he decided to wander down to the lake's edge, from where the fireworks were going to be launched. He sized up the situation and made the determination that the crowd was too close to the display. He went back to his family and told them to back up. They resisted his urging. Here is the account of his size-up, and how that effected his movement into a flow state.

> "I tried to explain to her [his wife], 'These
> things are too powerful. If one of these dropped
> down, it could blow up and hurt somebody.' No
> sooner than I tried to explain, one popped out
> about five feet from its sonotube, dropped back

down to the platform, and burst open. All the
four hundred thirty fireworks were surrounded
by boxes. He [the man designated to light the
fireworks] had set them up with the fuses all
hanging out of the boxes, so he could just light
them and throw them into the sonotubes. He
had tarps that were on two boxes. When the one
blew up, the ones he had on a rock wall right
behind him all started to go off. They were
blowing up and shooting towards the crowd.
When the first one blew up, it was like slow
motion. I watched and thought, 'This is going to
be interesting.' But when it burst open, all you
could see was this gigantic flash of flame. I
started yelling to everybody, 'Run, run, run!' I
turned around and grabbed my kids and started
running. It was like being in a war.

"My instinct was to run. Then I realized 'I've
got my whole family here.' I grabbed my kids...
As I did that, I noticed a tall propane canister
that they were using for cooking. I dove and
knocked over the canister. I then threw my son
behind a little doghouse. By this time,
everything had blown off."

In this situation, the trigger for McNamara was the initial
explosion and the instinct to save himself. Yet he was able to
prioritize his actions and take care of his family, as well as be
aware of other potential dangers (the propane canister).

Joel Kanasky's experience at the World Trade Center put him
in immediate danger. I asked him when flow happened for him.
He said,

"I think it's when you get into the magnitude of
it... Going on runs is no biggie. But when you
get there, and you start to assess, you realize
this is bad, and it's going to get a lot worse...
You know that you or others are not going to

make it. It doesn't happen every day... It just depends."

Child Involvement

Out of the 49 stories I collected in my doctoral study, 14 involved children. Gay Jones described an unresponsive baby call. When they arrived, the anomaly that Jones noticed was that the mother was *not* hysterical, as is usually the case with child involvement.

> "She was just standing out in the parking lot and pointing up to the room. Everything happened in a nanosecond. It was weird, because you usually hear the mom screaming before you even get off the rig. This mother appeared unconscious...

> "When we went up to the room, there was another weird vibe. There was a man in the apartment. He was just pacing back and forth. He pointed to the baby's room. When we ran into the bedroom, we saw this baby, who was maybe one-year old. The baby was unresponsive. I remember knowing immediately that this was not right. It turned out to be one of the first shaken baby syndrome incidences in my county."

Consciously Initiating Flow

How firefighters dealt with the trigger varied. While some participants recognized when they were game on, in the zone, or in the flow at the time, only one firefighter in my study said that she consciously decided to enter the flow state. In multiple stories, she told me the trigger for the flow state and then said, "I hit the kill switch," which enabled her to focus on the task at hand (one of the characteristics of flow) and not get caught up in emotions or the unfolding drama. Everyone else said that flow happened at an unconscious level.

There are five mechanisms of flow that must be in place for us to be able to consciously initiate flow, as shown in Figure 2: Knowledge of our own triggers of flow, preparation, physical readiness, mental alignment, and spiritual connection.

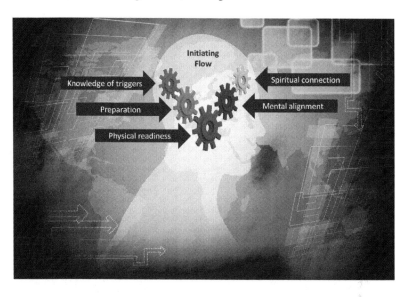

Figure 2: Five Mechanisms of Flow

Knowledge of Our Own Triggers

Most of us are not involved in situations where a child is in trouble or our safety is threatened, but we do experience things that are out of the ordinary. The triggers of flow are not the same from person to person. To be able to consciously initiate flow, you have to understand what puts you in a flow state. You can achieve this by paying attention when you recognize that you are in flow. Ask yourself, "What was I doing just prior to this feeling? What were conditions in my environment?"

Sometimes, flow comes from our decision to push ourselves a little harder through the activity, thereby introducing more challenges. This is the act of presencing. When you know what triggers flow for you, you can begin to put into place the conditions that bring about flow, thereby maximizing your flow experiences.

Preparation

Kahneman defines *cognitive strain* as being "affected by both the current level of effort and the presence of unmet demands."[26] This negatively affects creativity and intuition. Cognitive strain is mitigated through preparation.

Preparation is about readiness. People who understand how flow works spend the time to prepare themselves, even if preparation activities don't put them in a flow state.[27] Preparation refers to training and experience. It refers to taking care of the tools of your trade. It refers to rehearsal—repeating the activity until it is ingrained at a cellular level. This is what enables recognition-primed decision making. The activity is so familiar to you that when you are challenged by something out of the ordinary, you can continue to function at an optimal level with confidence.

Physical Readiness

Both physical strength and cardiovascular health contribute to our sense of overall well-being. Attention to physical fitness

---

[26] Kahneman, 2011

[27] Csikszentmihalyi, 2003

through play and exercise is essential to our ability to initiate flow states.[28]

While not all firefighters I know take the time to work out every day, most of them have some kind of physical regimen they follow, on and off the job. Their lives are in service to others. They understand that the concept of being in service to others means that they have to take care of themselves and their equipment first—not in a selfish way, but in a selfless way. Their outward focus is what drives them.

Mental Alignment

Flow requires a consolidation of attentional processes. Fragmentation of these processes prevents flow from occurring.[29] When we are mentally aligned, we are better able to be situationally aware. In other words, we are able to actively watch and assess so that we can respond in the best way possible, using "mental simulation."[30] The ability to react effectively requires feedback, active awareness, and low levels of inhibition, three common elements of flow. When people are in flow, they tend to lower their inhibitions when stressed.[31] When they are stressed, strategies that worked in the past may no longer be valid. This allows for the consideration of a variety of alternatives, based on perception and cognition. They reject the ideas that are not productive or feasible, and select those that appear to work for the situation. Conversely, people with high

---

[28] Seligman, 2002

[29] Csikszentmihalyi, 1990

[30] Klein, 1999

[31] Peat, 2008

levels of inhibition and low cognitive ability shut down in the face of stress when in intractible situations.[32]

Spiritual Connection

Alan Watts wrote about the Buddhist Middle Path, or Noble Eight-Fold Path of right understanding: right thought, right speech, right action, right livelihood, right effort, right mindfulness, and right concentration.[33] Firefighters exercise the sort of detached compassion Watts wrote about. Awareness is what facilitates their ability to do this.[34] Firefighters have a moral commitment to help others.[35] They have a duty to act, which refers to his or her responsibility to help others both on and off the job, because of their specialized training and expertise.[36]

When Flow Doesn't Happen

Not all emergency calls trigger flow states. Paige Colwell said she had considered why this is and "would love to know how to be able to reproduce them." She didn't believe it was the adrenaline rush. She has run many calls over the years; most are routine.

Critical events in the fire service are emergent in nature. That means that decisions need to be made concurrently, rather than sequentially. In the following story, Fire Chief Richard Kline didn't feel "on," either physically or psychologically. While he

---

[32] Peat, 2008; H. L. Thompson, 2010

[33] Watts, 2003

[34] Greenleaf, 1977

[35] Taylor & Wolin, 2002

[36] American Academy of Orthopaedic Surgeons, 2002

expressed some of the elements of flow, such as "I felt like I was in a slow-motion movie," he didn't feel that he was tuned in. He did a size-up, but it took him a while to recognize what was on fire. His instructions to the first trucks were not clear. He told them, "I want you to establish a water supply," rather than, "Here's your hydrant; I want you to lay a line in." He was not being direct with his crew, which led to questions and conjecture. This impacted the event, even though it ended well.

> "It's just that I had my B-game that particular early morning, [but] I didn't know it until after the fact. It doesn't happen that often, but every once in a while, I just don't have that flow coming to me. When I make a decision, I'm not looking at the implications of that decision... Oftentimes, based on your experiences and training and what you've seen and heard in the past, you subconsciously recognize the impact of that. Well, in this particular case, I didn't. The assignments to the crew were vague: 'We have a fire on the outside of the house.' 'Okay. Tell me more. What do you want us to do?' That wasn't done, and it should have been."

When they got back to the station, a couple of the crew came up to him and asked him if he was all right. They recognized that he wasn't on his A-game.

> "I said, 'Man, I felt like shit in terms of my decision making.' I told them how I didn't feel at ease with the event. They said, 'Yeah, we noticed that. You just seemed to struggle a little bit.' It can be transparent to some, if they know you and know what to expect from you. I thought that was kind of neat."

This last comment is very telling about those in the fire service. They take what could potentially be a negative and turn it into a positive.

> "We use this as a learning tool. After these critical events, we go back as a command staff, depending on the event, as a department, and critique them in terms of decision making and actions and impact of actions."

As discussed in the Mental Alignment section above, stress can cause people to shut down, especially when they have high levels of inhibition and low cognitive ability.[37] This was evident in a story told by David Rhodes, who was involved in the search and rescue of a number of children in a mobile home fire. The firefighters that had arrived before Rhodes' crew had put out the fire, "but smoke was boiling out the front door." He and his crew were able to crawl into the mobile home about five feet when the captain from the first company handed him a child and indicated that there were more. Rhodes took the child. He laid the child on the ground, so that the EMTs could start working on him. Rhodes then went back to the mobile home, as other firefighters were coming at him carrying more children. All of this happened within the first ten minutes of arriving on the scene. The highest ranking officer on the scene was a brand new lieutenant.

> "We kept hearing, 'there's more.' There were a lot of kids that stayed in this trailer. I looked at the lieutenant and said, 'Do you want me to go back? Or do I need to stay here? Or what?' [The lieutenant] was totally zoned out and gone. He didn't know what to say. He didn't know if he wanted me to start working on these kids. They

---

[37] Peat, 2008; H. L. Thompson, 2010

needed immediate attention, but if we didn't get the other ones out, they wouldn't have a chance. So, the decision that I had to make was: Do I take all my gear off and start working on this one kid or do I go back and help? [The lieutenant] put his hands on either side of his head, which is a classic sign of too much confusion. The bodies kept coming. He froze. He just lost it, and started walking away. He walked back to the station. He left. He never came back to our station again. He got psych evaluations and counseling. He got transferred, and ended up getting promoted a couple of years later. He passed away probably four or five years after that. He was young.

"I don't know if it was because the situation involved kids or what. He had handled other situations just fine. Maybe it was because he was the in-charge person, and there were too many decisions that had to be made all at once. I guess he needed a plan to tell him what to do instead of using what he had and just getting to work. He just couldn't take it, so he left. He just shut down."

Preparatory activities often don't trigger flow. For example, I know firefighters who are not particularly enamored with certain aspects of being prepared, such as maintaining equipment or doing heavy physical training (PT) early in the morning. However, they also know that if they are ready to respond physically with fully operational equipment—which will help facilitate a flow state—then those seemingly menial tasks are worthy of their time and energy.

On a personal level, I have learned that if I go to the gym early in the morning and work out for 45 minutes, I feel better during the day. My energy level is strong and my mind is sharp. In addition, there are the side benefits of lowering my cholesterol and evening out my blood pressure, so that I don't have to take medication. This enables my emotional and mental bandwidth to expand. I have "room" to put myself in challenging situations that stretch my skills—one of the preconditions of flow.

Conclusion

Either consciously or subconsciously, people naturally seek out flow experiences in their lives. Being in a flow state makes one feel authentic, giving the feeling that one is working at his or her highest potential. This is the essence of why flow matters. The stories collected in my research demonstrated a positive correlation between being in a flow state and making appropriate decisions. However, that correlation is dependent on training, preparation, and experience.

The firefighters I spoke with related that being in a flow state actually enhanced their abilities to respond appropriately. Training, preparation, and experience are staples in public service in varying degrees. The more leadership commits to training and preparation, the more likely the leader's team will experience flow when the situation warrants it.

There is a great deal of discussion in public service about situational awareness. Being consciously aware of your surroundings, of yourself in the moment, and of the other people involved in the situation enables the ability to consciously initiate flow.

Flow doesn't always happen. But when flow doesn't happen, training and experience help facilitate right decision making.

3 Flow-based Decision Making

"It was as if I had no real choice. It was not so much a decision about what I 'ought' to do—rather, I could not do otherwise. At this moment...one arrives at a point where freedom and destiny merge. It was at this point that my words became action."

—Joseph Jaworski

How flow impacts decision making and the ability to lead is dependent on the individual's level of confidence. Confidence is a function of training, experience, and preparation in the form of physical readiness, mental alignment, and spiritual connection. To accomplish this, the individual must be situationally aware at multiple levels. When all these aspects are in place, leadership happens—whether it is self-leadership or leadership of others.

Importance of Training and Experience

Most people can experience flow; however, you must begin with "a certain level of skill, training, and discipline."[38] Joel Kanasky attributed his ability to respond appropriately at the World Trade Center to his training: "Training and always being prepared gives you the ability to respond this way. It is that repetition."

The data collected in my doctoral study validated previous studies of firefighters and their ability to use "slides," or stories, to make decisions and to train others. Helen Graham, a wildland firefighter, told her stories using slides. For her, the slide concept itself represented a sense of control.

> "I see parallels in what you are talking about and in the way we train, lead, and make decisions in wildland firefighting. It comes from how the military Special Forces train in situation awareness. We emphasize a process of building what we call slides, as in a slide show. You take each situation that you have exposure to, where decisions were made, and you have the opportunity to evaluate outcomes.
>
> "A slide is a picture in your mind of the situation. The slide contains what happened in the situation, what it meant to you, how you lived through that situation, and how you looked back and evaluated the outcomes of the situation. Your slides become your repertoire for decision making.
>
> "We share our slides to prepare others who have not been in that situation. We teach our leaders

---

[38] Csikszentmihalyi, 1993

how to recognize what slides they have, which
ones they need to develop, and which ones they
can get from each other. We've been training on
that concept about ten or twelve years now.
That's how we do it. We pull those things out
quite readily now."

David Rhodes related a lesson from early in his career that
impacted how he changed his own process, and that he had
incorporated into his training of others. His crew responded to a
house fire with suspected entrapment of the people who lived
there. Rhodes sized up the situation and made his best estimate
of where the bedroom window would be. He knew to stomp on
the floor before entering a burning house through the window.
When he looked in, the floor appeared to be intact. He stomped
the floor. It held. He entered through the window and
immediately fell to the basement. He had stomped on the floor
joist. The floor itself had burned from underneath, but the
carpet was still intact. As a result of this experience, he
consciously changed his knowledge base to remind himself to
test multiple locations before entering the building. He also
modified the training he did with others, telling them to stomp
in multiple locations.

I asked another firefighter how training factors into her flow
experience. She told me that training only goes so far. Actually
doing the work is what built the confidence she needed to be
successful.

"Training, I think, goes to the initial doing of
something and then once I've done it a few
times, it is experience and repetition, and
recognition of previous situations... You can
practice and get your required two hundred IV
sticks in paramedic school and in the emergency
rooms. Does that teach you how to do it when

> you're straddling somebody going down the
> road in the back of an ambulance, and they are
> fighting you or they are seizing? No. It's just
> having done it."

A fire chief in a small volunteer department told me a story about a late night house fire in a rural area, when he had staffing and equipment issues. In addition, there was a lack of supervising officers. He had to rely on mutual aid officers (i.e., officers outside his own jurisdiction), but because he had "brought his A-game," he was able to "manage all of those inputs coming at me all at once, and prioritize and categorize them, and then make my decisions based on that...the only way you do that is through experience and training."

These examples bear out what Csikszentmihalyi found in his studies:

> Universally, optimal experiences are reported to
> occur within sequences of activities that are
> goal-directed and bounded by rules—activities
> that require the investment of psychic energy,
> and that could not be done without the
> appropriate skills.[39]

Klein found that intuition can be trained by expanding an individual's experience base. He suggested the use of realistic scenarios, in which the trainer can stop action, change direction, or use concurrent, time-sensitive situations "to develop a sense of typicality."[40] The participants in my study confirmed these findings. "What gets you in a flow is how you have been trained, along with what your knowledge, skills, and abilities are."

---

[39] Csikszentmihalyi, 1990
[40] Klein, 1998

Tunnel Vision vs. Hyper-vision

Without this training and experience, being in a flow state can actually be detrimental. Because firefighters work in an environment where time is scarce, they have to be very focused on the task at hand. This means that anything deemed extraneous to the task falls to the wayside. In other words, when you are concentrating on the task at hand, you might miss things that could be potentially dangerous. In their book *Scarcity: The New Science of Having Less and How it Defines Our Lives*, Mullainathan and Shafir refer to this phenomenon as "tunnelling."[41]

This idea is supported by the firefighter in my study who had the least amount of experience. He commented that "being in the zone" gives him tunnel vision, because he is concentrating so hard on the task at hand. When he experienced flow, he was afraid of missing something. He told a story about being in a burning house where there was a wood-burning stove chimney box above him. The stove was gone, but the chimney box was still there. He wasn't aware of it in the moment, but saw it after the fire was put out when he was involved in the cleanup. He realized then that it could have come down on top of him during the fire and killed him. He filed that experience as a slide for future reference. This is where experience enhances future decision making.

> "The longer you are in the job, the tunnel vision doesn't get as tight. In the flow, tunnel vision happens. No matter how much you train for it. Maybe when you have thirty years on, you can get even better with it. But when you are in it, you're missing other things."

---

[41] Mullainathan & Shafir, 2013

Another firefighter disputed the idea of tunnel vision.

> "When I get there, it's like hyperfocus. I'm completely in tune with the situation and what has to happen next. When I say hyperfocus, I don't mean that I have tunnel vision... You have to be doing what you are doing, preparing to intubate, while asking family members, 'When did you last see them awake? What is their medical history?' All of this is going on at the same time. You have to be aware of family members and how they are reacting with the overall situation. Is there anything dangerous in the house? Are there signs that this could be a drug overdose? What other things? It's not tunnel vision; it's being in tune with the entire situation. What kicks you into that, I don't know. But, I think, that's where it starts."

One California firefighter talked about her experiences as a firefighter, an apparatus operator/engineer, a captain, and as a battalion chief. "I'm thinking of situations at each of those levels, where you just take a picture and you look and you see everything. You see everything all at once. I would call that the zone."

Commitment to Learning

Firefighters are committed to learning. Firefighters read after-action incident reports. They discuss incidents when they go back to the station. Some have told me arguments often occur about what happened on scene, because the point of view was different for each firefighter. A seemingly minor difference of being on the hose versus being on the nozzle can change the firefighter's perspective dramatically, depending on the incident. Talking through these different points of view creates a three-dimensional picture of what really happened. Chief Richard Kline commented,

> "Most of the incident commanders that are worth their salt in the fire service analyze their actions, because they want to. Number one, they want to protect their people, but also protect the public. The only way to do that is to learn from your mistakes. We're human, so we're error-prone, just by our nature, so you are going to make mistakes. You have to learn from those. The better incident commanders that you interview are going to admit to that. They'll say, 'Yep. I screwed up, but I learned from it.'

> "I go back and do a mental simulation of what happened. Sometimes I write it down; sometimes I don't, but I say, 'Boy, if this ever happens again, I learned from this, and here's my different action, or I'll take a different approach to the event.'"

How Flow Enhances Decision Making

At any given moment, there are an infinite number of choices to act or not act.[42] The process of choice is a conscious bifurcation—or point of departure—from the conditions an individual is experiencing. This is the point at which awareness and action merge. Fragmentation within the individual arises when you make reactive choices as a result of inattention to feelings and lack of attention to actions.[43] Choice is determined by the totality of significance in the moment. How we choose includes both explicit and tacit knowledge.[44] The emphasis on

---

[42] Peat, 2008

[43] Bohm, 1980

[44] Bohm, 2003

continuous training in the firefighter culture is based on minimizing reactive choices.[45]

Size-up: Creative Suspension of Choice

In his book, *Gentle Action: Bringing Creative Change to a Turbulent World*, David Peat presents a concept he calls "creative suspension," which is a "voluntary act, on the part of an individual or organization, to suspend, if only for a moment, a normal 'knee-jerk' reaction to rush in and 'help' or 'put things right.'" Creative suspension involves stopping, even if only for an instant, to evaluate the situation—to do triage, or in the language of firefighting, do a size-up—before making the decision on how to proceed. "However, creative suspension is not the act of 'doing nothing.' It is an active form of watchfulness and assessment, in order to take the most effective action as quickly as possible."[46] Klein refers to this as "situation awareness...[which] can be formed rapidly, through intuitive matching of features, or deliberately, through mental simulation."[47]

Creative suspension facilitates a change in phase space in self-organizing systems, creating a space of all possible actions. As an event or system emerges, employing creative suspension has the effect of changing the dynamics of that system and making possible the reorganization of that system, as old feedback loops are abandoned and new ones temporarily created. Creative suspension opens up possibilities that may not have been available in the earlier iteration of that system or event.

---

[45] International Association of Fire Chiefs and National Fire Protection Association [IAFCNFPA], 2009

[46] Peat, 2008

[47] Klein, 1999

Employing creative suspension effectively requires feedback, active awareness, and low levels of inhibition, three common elements of flow. Most people have "a coping mechanism called 'latent inhibition,' which acts to inhibit or filter out most of the messages we receive and process only those that are necessary to our survival at any given moment."[48]

People with low levels of inhibition are able to be more creative in their decision-making processes because they are open to more possibilities. High levels of inhibition lead to rigidity, which causes individuals and organizations to be less flexible about change, even when change would lead to a more optimal outcome.

Thompson describes this phenomenon in terms of high versus low cognitive ability. High cognitive people are more likely to be receptive of feedback and "rely on themselves to provide missing information, look for more novel information, and search across more domains to find information." High cognitive leaders are more in tune with themselves and their relationships. They recognize when they are communicating with others who do not have the same level of cognitive ability, and make the effort to ensure understanding in their communications. People with low cognitive ability "tend to use few dimensions when processing stimuli...tend to contrast themselves with others and are less open to feedback...[and] tend to have a relatively narrow set of interests and knowledge domains."[49]

---

[48] Peat, 2008

[49] H. L. Thompson, 2010

The Action/Inaction Continuum

How you respond in stressful situations lies on an action/inaction continuum. This continuum, illustrated in Figure 3, correlates to your level of rigidity. At the far end of the continuum, at maximum rigidity, you are totally committed to mission and policy to the extent that no matter what happens, you continue to make decisions as you always have. At the next level, when you recognize the hugeness and complexity of the issues or problem, but still hold on to rigid ideas and practices, paralysis can set in. Moving toward the action or less rigid end of the continuum, you are aware of the situation and are willing to let go of inhibitions, but you lack creativity or are unsuccessful in mitigating the situation; you will get stuck reorganizing the system over and over, implementing unsuccessful strategy after unsuccessful strategy. On the action or most flexible end of the continuum, you are open to feedback, and "with sufficient creativity and intelligence, [you] can adopt new, appropriate and possibly even unanticipated strategies...[facilitating the ability] to respond to new situations in sustainable ways."

Highly flexible people do not seek to predict and control situations and events, but rather allow situations and events to emerge, making decisions that are appropriate to the moment in response to continuous feedback. This correlates to the idea of the merging of action and awareness that occurs in a flow state. Leaders rise out of the necessity for specific talents and knowledge required in the situation. People with tacit knowledge—achieved through training and experience—are better equiped to know when the time is right to act. Artists, for example, often speak of their creative process as a "holding" within themselves until the time is right for expression.

Figure 3: Action/Inaction Continuum

Gentle action is action "that does not desire to dominate and control, but seeks balance and good order and is based on respect for nature and society." Gentle action occurs when you make appropriate decisions in response to your sensitivity "to the dynamics of their surrounding environment... Gentle action is subtle in nature so that a minimal intervention, intelligently made, can result in a major change or transformation."[50]

Peat likens gentle action to the soliton wave phenomenon in physics. A soliton wave is caused by nonlinear effects, which cause wavelets produced by an initial action (e.g., tossing a stone in a river) to bind with one another to create a continuous wave instead of dissipating after traveling outwards from the

[50] Peat, 2008

point of origin. Examples of this phenomenon exist in weather patterns ("In 1951 a mass of cold air around 100 miles long traveled across Kansas at a speed of 12 mph for several hundred miles") and in water ("the 'bore' of the Amazon River can be as high as 25 feet and travel for over 500 miles without breaking apart"). This effect can also be seen in superconductors where

> [...] the electrical current will continue to flow indefinitely. The reason for this is that at sufficiently low temperatures an extremely weak attraction between electrons is moving in a totally coherent way as if, to use a colorful image, they had one mind. No longer do the moving electrons interfere with atoms in the lattice, they just flow past them leaving them undisturbed. In this way, the resistance normally experienced by an electrical current simply vanishes and the current continues to flow indefinitely.[51]

Gentle action could be construed as a consciousness-based soliton wave within society, where "individuals are bound together through a shared meaning, so that a large number of tiny individual gestures harmonize together to form a great social movement."[52] In other words, each individual within the system has an impact on the dynamics within the system. "The collective is enfolded within the individual and the individual within the collective." High cognitive ability, low inhibition, and high emotional intelligence enable the individual to act with confidence from a place of knowing.

Creative suspension and gentle action facilitate the ability to look at the world in fresh, new ways, opening the possibilities for moving with the system involved rather than resisting it,

---

[51] *Ibid*

[52] *Ibid.*

much the same way some martial arts use the momentum of your opponent against him or her. The choice to employ creative suspension to effect gentle action can happen in the blink of an eye, based on instinct and recognition. When we jump to conclusions rapidly with minimal information, we are using the unconcious mental processes called the "adaptive unconscious."[53] We see patterns in situations and behaviors that we can relate back to previous training and experience. Gladwell refers to this as "thin-slicing." Relationships, systems, and events all have distinctive patterns. We gravitate toward decisions that are known to have had successful results in the past. However, when the situation is new, unexpected, or unfamiliar, we are less likely to respond with confidence.[54]

Decision Making Models

We tend to think of decision making as better done when we have as much information as possible, so that we can weigh out all the alternatives before making an intelligent decision. Business schools and other management training programs teach some variation of the seven-step method shown in Figure 4: (a) identify the problem; (b) gather information; (c) analyze the situation and redefine the problem; (d) generate alternatives; (e) evaluate alternatives; (f) select and implement a solution; and (g) evaluate results.

However, most people do not make decisions this way, even if there is a great deal of information and plenty of time to evaluate options. This kind of analysis is not practical in most settings.[55] Lehrer points out that "Even though we are defined

---

[53] Gladwell, 2005

[54] Klein, 1999

[55] Klein, 1999; H. L. Thompson, 2010

by our decisions, we are often completely unaware of what's happening inside our heads during the decision-making process." In critical situations, emotions take over. Experience facilitates accurate reliance on emotion, which leads to right action.[56]

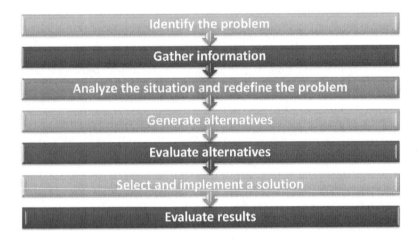

Identify the problem

Gather information

Analyze the situation and redefine the problem

Generate alternatives

Evaluate alternatives

Select and implement a solution

Evaluate results

Figure 4: Traditional Decision Making Process

There are two types of strategies for making decisions: (a) intuitive and (b) rational.

> Intuitive decisions are made quickly, automatically, emotionally, and mostly unconsciously, and they tend to be of a routine or emergency nature... Rational decisions tend to be much more complex and more conscious, take longer, and use more structured processes than intuitive decision making.[57]

People tend to use the intuitive decision strategy when time pressure is greater, when they have more experience, when conditions are dynamic, and when goals are ill-defined. We are

---

[56] Lehrer, 2009

[57] H. L. Thompson, 2010

more likely to use a rational decision strategy when there is a need for justification, conflict resolution, optimization, and greater computational complexity. However, most people, even when using a rational strategy, will use mental simulation to compare courses of action.

> We will be more likely to compare options when faced with an unfamiliar situation. The reason is that a lack of experience will prevent us from generating reasonable options, or will at least reduce our confidence in the options we do generate.[58]

In the mid-1980s, Klein conducted extensive empirical research on firefighters. He defines *naturalistic decision making* as "the study of how people use their experience to make decisions in field settings."[59] The features of a natualistic decision making (NDM) setting are time pressure, high stakes, experienced decision makers, inadequate information (information is missing, ambiguous, or erroneous), ill-defined goals, poorly defined procedures, cue learning (e.g., higher-level goals, stress), dynamic conditions, and team coordination.

As a result of Klein's research, he was able to codify what he calls the Recognition-Primed Decision (RPD) Model, illustrated in Figure 5. RPD was developed based on field studies of the way that experienced personnel actually make decisions. The model explains how you can use experience to react rapidly and make good decisions without having to contrast options. The model has been tested and supported by research teams working in a variety of settings.

---

[58] Klein, 1999

[59] *Ibid*

RPD is not the same as NDM. The difference is that RPD is used by people with experience who use mental simulation, a deliberate, conscious process that helps "make sense of events and form an explanation." We recognize patterns that remind us of previous events. "Usually we will scan each explanation to see if there are elements that do not seem plausible, so we can reject the less likely ones and keep the best." By constructing mental simulations, also known as story models, or slides, for each iteration of experience, we are better able to respond quickly to events. Klein found that "fireground commanders showed that when they did need to evaluate a course of action, they used the strategy of mental simulation."[60]

Figure 5: Klein's Recognition-Primed Decision (RPD) Model[61]

Most studies of decision making in the fire service have focused on high-ranking chief officers, who are making command decisions on the fireground and often arrive on the scene after initial decisions have been made by lower-ranking company officers. There have been very few studies that focus on company officers' decision making. These are the firefighters to

---

[60] Klein, 1999

[61] Used with permission.

first arrive on the scene, and make command decisions prior to the arrival of the chief officer. My own study focused on a broad range of experience and rank, from on-the-ground firefighters to chiefs of departments, large and small. David Wall, Division Director of the Georgia Fire Academy, is currently working on the first study of company officer decision making to "explore the cognitive barriers to having good situation awareness with the goal of increasing the quality of decisions made in those NDM environments."[62] This study will contribute to the body of knowledge in the area of decision making in a way that will inform the development of training for company officers, and increase their ability to use the RPD Model.

It is important to be aware of your feelings in each moment, thereby minimizing potentially negative consequences.[63] Therefore, when you are able to imagine a positive outcome to life's challenges and incorporate experience and training to facilitate that imagined outcome, you will be more likely to make choices consistent with that positive image. Your expectations can become "self-fulfilling prophecies."[64] Bad decisions are most often made because of "inexperience, lack of knowledge, or poor judgment." The most critical component of good, consistent decision making is learned ability: knowledge, training, and experience coupled with the awareness that everything is a system, requiring the continuous processing of feedback and other information that may not necessarily be available in a sequential manner.[65]

---

[62] Wall, 2016

[63] Bohm, 2003

[64] Lehrer, 2009

[65] H. L. Thompson, 2010

Csikszentmihalyi observed that flow states allow an individual to retain control of his or her psychic energy, while not necessarily being aware of what happens in the body or mind.[66] Paige Colwell felt that being in a flow state enabled her to make all the right decisions, when she felt one with the activity. There was no planning or vetting of options. She just acted.

> "It can happen trying to start an IV on a critical patient who is in a car with a head injury and who is moving all over the place. It happens in situations where I have one shot, or when something desperately has to happen right now... It is hyperfocus. I don't know what it is, but everything slows down. 'Hummingbird's wings' is the best description I can tell you. It's like I can see each individual beat. It just happens. It flows—that's a good word for it."

Rich Gasaway described being in the flow as having the "command mindset."

> "From the time I get the call until the call is done, I am 'game on' to the incident... I try very hard to block other things out of my mind and focus entirely on the incident to be managed. It's like my mind shifts gears into a different dimension. I develop a hypervigilance to my surroundings, and see and hear things that otherwise I might not have seen or heard."

Mitigating the Effects of Stress

While my study indicated a connection between flow and decision making, emotional and cognitive intelligence and resilience are also necessary for effective decision making. However, stress can have a significant impact on decision

---

[66] Csikszentmihalyi, 1990

making, even in a flow state. Because you are concentrating on the task at hand, the stress, rather than throwing you into flow, may actually prevent flow from happening, as we talked about in Chapter 2.

To mitigate stress, you need to also have stress management capacity, cognitive intelligence, and resilient emotional intelligence. H. L. Thompson's work, illustrated in Figure 6, offers "seven best practices—Awareness, Rest, Support, Exercise, Nutrition, Attitude, and Learning (ARSENAL)—[to] build capacity in these three key factors and contribute to developing and maintaining a stress resilient system."[67]

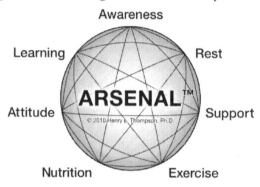

Figure 6: H. L. Thompson's ARSENAL[68]

By strengthening your ARSENAL, you minimize your anxiety and resulting stress, which helps you concentrate on the task at hand. There is a certain feeling of confidence that occurs when you are rested and feeling good, both mentally and physically. When you have had the right training and experience, decisions come easily.

The first best practice in Thompson's model is awareness. Firefighters often talk about situational awareness in their

---

[67] Thompson, 2010

[68] Used with permission.

stories. When concentrating on the task at hand and through observation in each moment, they are able to allow awareness and action to merge. This is true not only when they are fighting fire, but even in their interactions at the firehouse and in their personal lives. Learning to be situationally aware is a skill that can be learned, practiced, and improved over time with training and experience.

Situation Awareness

Situation awareness (SA) theory came into being around 25 years ago, in the field of human factors. There has been a great deal of SA research, discussion, cynicism, and criticism during that time. Endsley's 1995 Model of Situation Awareness is the de facto model that is most often cited. Endsley has dissected the concept of SA into three non-linear levels, and described to the nth degree what they all mean in multiple publications. Her level of granularity makes the process of situation awareness sound complex and cumbersome. The more granular she gets with her explanations, the more other researchers criticize her approach—often using their own research to dispute her model, using different words to describe basically the same concepts. (Such is the life of the researcher.) If you are interested in reading more about this ongoing discussion of what constitutes SA, see *Journal of Cognitive Engineering and Decision Making*, Volume 9, Number 1, March 2015. The entire issue is dedicated to this topic.

While this level of discourse is necessary to be able to develop subsequent training, I find it impractical to implement on a day-to-day, moment-by-moment basis. When you are in flow, you don't actually think about the mechanics of decision making. While the steps contained in the Endsley model are within the decision making process, they happen in a nanosecond.

Prior to Endsley, in the early 1950s, there was a U.S. Airforce fighter pilot named Lt. Col. John Boyd, who looked at improving the effectiveness of fighter pilots. Boyd was a fearless fighter pilot. He loved the fighter pilot role. With each subsequent flight, he evaluated his learning. He knew that to be better, he had to systematize the process. Ultimately, he realized that to be the most effective while he was flying, he had to first observe, orient himself and his plane, decide on the best course of action, and then actually act. He called this OODA (Observe, Orient, Decide, and Act). To be the most effective, he had to rapidly repeat this process over and over. This process is known as OODA Loop.

System 1 and System 2 Thinking

More recently, Kahneman has reported his own model in his seminal book *Thinking, Fast and Slow*. In his model, the mind is divided into two systems he calls System 1 and System 2. System 1 operates instinctively and spontaneously, without a sense of intention; System 2 allocates attention toward more complex situations, when the consideration of choice is involved.

System 1 tends to be reductionist. System 1 thinking makes us see the world as uncomplicated and predictable. This can result in "narrow framing" of our perception of events, causing us to limit the number of choices to a few, rather than enabling us to look at the broader picture, which may yield many more possibilities. Loss aversion, coupled with narrow framing, can be extremely costly. It is in our nature to frame events narrowly, because it is easier to manage the choices.

System 2 assists in "broad framing," which allows us to see the complexity in the event and a broader range of options and possibilities. Experience facilitates broad framing. Adopting preferences for risky choices, such as codifying standard operating procedures and predetermining responses to difficult decisions, helps mitigate narrow framing.[69]

Here is an example of the impact of adopting a predetermined response tactic. For years, since the 1940s and 1950s, firefighters have been taught to fight fire from the unburned side and to push the fire back. This training was based on the fact that structural layouts were more compartmentalized and the contents were made of natural fibers, and, therefore, took longer (up to 28 minutes) for conditions to deteriorate to flash-over stage. This is known as a "legacy fire load."

Modern day construction is much different because many of the building layouts are large and open and the contents are petroleum-based. In more recent construction, a flash over can occur in as little as three minutes. The petroleum-based contents can consume the oxygen more rapidly than before and create conditions that are more lethal in less time. In other words, occupants of modern homes have from two to five minutes to evacuate a home; occupants of older homes have up to half an hour to evacuate. Given that it takes an average of seven to ten minutes for the fire department to respond to a call, research is showing that it is important to get water on the fire as quickly as possible from any direction and not specifically or only from the unburned side.

---

[69] Kahneman, 2011

In addition, personal protection equipment (PPE) was not, then, what it is today. PPE has improved substantially over time to include Self-Contained Breathing Apparatus (SCBA) that protects the firefighter's respiratory system from the toxic atmosphere. When fighting a legacy file load without SCBA, cooling down the structure prior to entry was also a common tactic based on keeping firefighters safe. As PPE got better and better, fighting fire became more aggressive, and firefighters would position hoses and fire streams inside the structure between the fire and the occupant to prevent the spread of fire toward the trapped individuals.

The researchers of Underwriters Laboratories' Firefighters Safety Research Institute (UL) have teamed up with experts in the fire service to study fire behavior in more recent construction. These studies have shown that it is important to apply water and attack the fire in the structure from the location that gets water on the fire in the fastest manner.

In the past, firefighters were taught that venting the structure meant cooling the structure for victims. However, adding air to modern day structures has the potential to actually increase the heat in the structure, putting trapped victims at risk. The UL studies have shown that, because fires are often oxygen deficient, there needs to be a coordinated effort to put water on the fire just as you open the structure for ventilation.

There is now supporting evidence, thanks to research, that cooling down the structure before entry is a sound tactic. However, these studies also emphasize that every situation is different. There is no one way to respond that works in every situation. Knowledge of the situation, fire behavior, and structure construction facilitate the appropriate response.

Firefighters still need to be aware that the specific tactics to use in an incident remain very situational.

It is up to individual departments to set policy and provide training that will help develop good decision makers. Deviation from the policy may occur at the discretion of the incident commander, with good reason. However, for the most part, this will help mitigate System 1, narrow-focus decision making. In many departments, this will involve a culture shift.

My Own Lesson in Situation Awareness

I observed my first Georgia Smoke Diver training in November 2011. It was early in the week. The candidates were learning how to use thermal imaging cameras in a smoke-filled burn building. Smoke Daddy David Rhodes (GSD #339) asked me if I wanted to go into the burn building. At first, I said, "No." But then I thought about it. How would I ever really know what they experience, if I didn't suit up and go in? I changed my mind and said, "Yes." The instructors had me in full gear before I could protest. Into the burn building I went, with one of the instructors, Captain Charlie Long (GSD #552).

Everything I had been hearing from all the firefighters in my doctoral study came at me in a rush. I had 70 pounds of gear on my body. At the time, I was not in good physical shape. I felt completely encumbered. All my senses were stripped away. The mask prevented me from tasting or smelling. I couldn't see for all the smoke. I couldn't feel anything because of the gloves. I couldn't hear, because the noise in the burn building was confusing. In a building that is burning, firefighters have told me, the noise can be deafening.

While I am not generally claustrophobic, I felt like I was closed in. I realized that my being frightened was causing me to breathe air too fast. I wasn't in the building 30 seconds before I said, "Charlie, I have to leave." He said, "No. No. Look through your TIC (thermal imaging camera). What do you see?" I looked. I could see other firefighters through the smoke. I couldn't see them without the camera.

Charlie then said, "Look down through the TIC. What do you see?" I looked down at an angle and saw another firefighter, but this was confusing, because of the angle I was looking. Charlie said, "That's your reflection in a mirror. Now look over there. What do you see?" I told him it looked like a hole. He said, "That's the hallway. Let's go down to the burn room."

We made our way to the room where the fire was burning. Charlie told me to look through the TIC to get the temperature reading. At eye level, the temperature was a little over 300 degrees Fahrenheit. He then told me to point the camera to the ceiling and take another reading. The TIC read over 600 degrees Fahrenheit (still cool, by firefighters' standards). I felt my internal body temperature begin to rise. Fear overtook me again.

I said, "Charlie, I need to leave." Charlie said, "Okay. But we can't go back the way we came. Others have come in behind us. We have to go down the stairs to go out." I was near panic at this point. I said, not so calmly, "Down the stairs!! Are you crazy!?" He calmly said, "No. No. Look through the TIC. What do you see?" I said, "Another hallway." He said, "Now, look down. What do you see?" I looked. It appeared to be a hole in the floor. He said, "Those are the stairs." I suddenly realized the amazing dangers firefighters face on a daily basis, never knowing if the next step will have them plunging into darkness to their deaths.

I made my way down the stairs slowly and carefully, and then out of the building. In all, I spent a total of 15 minutes in the burn building.

Long was an amazing coach. As I turned inward in fear, he refocused me outward. The urge to submit to a panicked state, to rip off my face mask, was huge, but Long helped me resist. That is how many firefighters die in fires, he told me. When I exited, my paradigm had changed dramatically. It is one thing to listen to people tell you their stories. It is another thing to experience what they mean by awareness.

The takeaway was that in emergency situations, firefighters must be situationally aware of themselves (internally), their surroundings, the dynamics of the fire or other relevant variables (individual people, crowds, weather conditions, construction of the building, etc.), and also be able to conduct a search for victims, if necessary. Every incident is different. And yet, there are repeating patterns within each incident that, over time, enable firefighters to act in a way that facilitates their ability to respond in the best way possible. However, they must be willing and able to constantly train, learn about past incidents, and unemotionally deconstruct, discuss, and evaluate incidents immediately following the action with fellow first responders. This enables them to learn what happened (from others' perspectives) and to determine what they might have done differently to affect the best outcome.

Conclusion

Flow-based decision making is effective if you have had repetitive, focused training. Situation awareness and the ability to make meaning of moment-to-moment feedback dictate your response to what is happening around you. When you find yourself in a situation you don't recognize, your training enables you to focus on the unfamiliar elements of the situation. Training helps you execute those tasks that are necessary to get through the situation, while freeing up your cognitive ability to problem solve.

However, it is important to also factor in the effects of stress, your ability and willingness to act, and emotional and cognitive capacity. If you or your organization is in a constant reactive state of being, the abilities to focus on the task at hand, to be open to possibility and creativity, and to act appropriately for the situation are all compromised.

The more experiences you have, the less likely you will experience tunnel vision. While focusing on the task at hand is a characteristic of flow, the more experiences you encounter, the more likely it is that focusing on the task at hand means that you are able to take in everything that is important to that task in a profound and holistic way, what many firefighters call "hyper-vision."

Experiences are not limited to personal experience. When an organization fosters knowledge sharing, you can learn from the experiences of others. This removes the time boundaries established by linear experiences and facilitates exponential growth of everyone on the team. This requires fostering of a learning culture, free of naming and blaming, and a commitment to life-long learning on the part of individuals as well as the organization.

4 Flow-based Leadership

"True leadership is not about superiority, position, or prestige. It's about revealing and releasing the potential of those around you. Leadership is not about the power of one, but facilitating the greatness of many."

—Brett and Kate McKay

The intersection of flow and leadership is a powerful place. The leader who is in a flow state is hyperaware of the environment, outwardly focused, and in tune with the team involved in resolution. The flow-based leader makes a conscious effort to ensure that the team operates in a flow state by allowing them to evolve in an organic way, while maintaining constant vigilance. This provides the ability to guide the team through the subtle and not-so-subtle changes that happen very quickly in emergent incidents.

Leadership Styles

Volumes have been written about leadership and all the different variations of leading. Higher education offers leadership degrees at all levels. Leadership has become a field of study. Leadership theories abound: authentic leadership, transformative leadership, transactional leadership, Renewed Darwinian Leadership, Leadership Theory in the Perspective of Kierkegaard's Philosophy, servant leadership, responsible leadership, and followership, just to name a few. Dozens of conferences and workshops are available worldwide for developing leaders, in every discipline and industry segment. We discuss, ad nauseam, whether leaders are born or made, and whether one form of leadership is better than another.

I have observed every type of leader in my research in the fire service. I would argue that there is no right or wrong way to lead. You have to find the leadership style that works for you, for the situation in which you find yourself. This requires self-knowledge and situational awareness.

According to the International Association of Fire Chiefs and the National Fire Protection Association, "Fire fighters are aggressive, action-oriented people who also can be compulsive. It is important that [fire officers] develop a command presence in order to focus the efforts of this action-oriented team."[70] The ability to bring order to the chaos requires a very specific leadership style. Incident commanders and other commanding officers must demonstrate the ability to lead by remaining calm; communicating clearly, honestly, and concisely; and consistently making right decisions. Remaining true to this leadership style instills trust.[71]

In emergent situations, firefighters have to be attuned to the dynamics of the system. For example, doing a size-up is a

---

[70] IAFCNFPA, 2006

[71] *Ibid*

collaborative effort. As a leader, you have to rely on your team to report what they observe. Team members need to take on the role of responsible leadership to ensure the reporting of a complete picture about which appropriate decisions can be made. However, as the scene changes, the fire officer must be able to adjust his or her leadership style from collaborative to autocratic instantaneously in the face of danger. In other words, everyone involved must be a leader, but also be aware enough to know when it is necessary and appropriate to be a follower in an instant.

The current effort to implement crew resource management (CRM), which came out of the aviation industry, encourages leaders to empower those who report to them to be more forthcoming when they disagree with a decision.

> CRM is a flexible, systemic method for optimizing human performance in general, and increasing safety in particular, by (1) recognizing the inherent human factors that cause errors and the reluctance to report them, (2) recognizing that in complex, high risk endeavors, teams rather than individuals are the most effective fundamental operating units, and (3) cultivating and instilling customized, sustainable and team-based tools and practices that effectively use all available resources to reduce the adverse impacts of those human factors.[72]

Making the shift from a pseudo-militaristic reporting structure to a more collaborative environment like CRM is difficult for many people and organizational cultures, especially those who enjoy the role of having power over others. However, at the end of the day, the ultimate goal is that everyone goes home safely.

---

[72] Safer Healthcare, 2016

Implementing CRM does not mean giving up command structure. If you are the person in charge on an incident, no matter what your rank, you must be able to shift from a collaborative leadership style to an autocratic leadership style in a heartbeat. This involves being secure enough in yourself to be willing to make decisions that will upset or even anger those with whom you are working.

Ben Barksdale was involved in multiple efforts on September 11, 2001 at the Pentagon. One endeavor was shoring up the floor to prevent collapse. Barksdale saw a real potential for danger, and did not hesitate to exert his authority. However, he did it in such a way as to minimize the perception of autocratic rule.

> "We brought in about a half million dollars in lumber—six by sixes (6X6s). They were twelve feet in length. They cut them in half so they were each six feet long. They built what we call crib towers. You just stack them like Lincoln Logs from floor to ceiling, and then you wedge it in at the top. You have to work in a safe zone as you are building the crib towers. The safe zone is that area radiating out from the crib tower where it is safe to work, where the force exerted by the ceiling is stabilized by the crib tower. This is called the cone of force. You know the safe zone by calculating how much force is being exerted by the ceiling on each tower.

> "I realized that the team that was building the towers was working outside of the safe zone, as it built each successive tower. This increased the chance of a collapse. I stopped them for the simple reason of safety. They were angry that I had stopped them, because they felt that they were fine, but I knew what forces that crib

tower generates. They needed to stay within the guidelines.

"I was commanding this team, but I didn't address the whole group. I just addressed the captain of the team. I told him, 'You need to tailor back and work within the zone.' The captain told the team, 'The chief says we can't work outside the zone.' That pissed them off, because they knew where it came from. They were working with a sense of urgency, 'Let's hurry up,' but it could have been disastrous if the ceiling had fallen in."

In this situation, Barksdale knew he needed to command appropriate action from the team, but he exhibited restraint and showed respect for the team leadership. This communication style instills trust and respect.

Being in a command role is like walking a tight wire. Any little thing might tip emotions or other dynamics in a way that is detrimental to the overall outcome. Followers and leaders alike must trust and respect one another to be effective in these emergent events. This is true in both time-compressed events and situations not constrained by time.

Example of an Event Not Constrained by Time

When Mary Beth Michos was hired into the Prince William County, Virginia Fire and Rescue Department (PWCDFR) as its new fire chief in 1994, she was told she was hired to change the culture. There had only been one chief there for 30 years before her. The previous chief had been a good chief; he did a lot of good things for the department. He hired a lot of good people, but he had decided it was time to retire.

At that time, there were no chiefs' schools. Fire chiefs had to do their best to put into practice what they had learned over the years as a supervisor and leader. However, until someone found himself or herself in that position, he or she had no idea what it was like to run a fire department.

Within the first few weeks, Michos noticed there was no teamwork whatsoever. People were competitive; there was very little collaboration taking place. The department was in a sorry state. She decided to bring in a consultant, who was a Deming follower and worked with quality control, to conduct a one-day retreat and attempt to build a team.

Michos' team met with Joe (the consultant) over dinner to plan the retreat. She hadn't given a lot of thought to what he was going to do prior to this meeting. He said he was going to help the team identify what was important. On the day of the retreat, Joe took Michos' team through a process that, by the end of the day, identified their organizational values. This was a very new concept to Michos. Her subsequent research led her to believe that this had never been done in the fire service. She learned a lot about the process of clarifying how her department wanted to be perceived.

She asked Joe afterward, "Now that we have had this retreat, what do we do?" She realized that, by identifying what was important to her as a leader, what was important to the department, going through a process to validate those values, and trying to live those values, she could change the organizational culture. She assimilated the values that her team chose for the department to live by into her own thinking, saying, "Over a period of time, as I changed as a leader and began to believe and use this concept, the culture changed."

Her team really focused on operationalizing the values they identified. She cited the values in her communications to people. When her team had to make decisions, they used the values as a measurement. They asked themselves, "Does this fit within our values?" They monitored each other to make sure the decisions they were making—the things they were doing—fell in line with those values. Over a period of time, as she changed as a leader and began to believe in and use this concept, the culture changed.

Michos went the additional mile to validate the changes in her department about seven years later, when she had some students from a Master's program at George Mason University come in and use an "appreciative inquiry process" to reassess the values. To Michos' surprise, the students discovered PWCDFR had evolved to a very different set of values.

Their original values were all focused on "I" and "me," and the insecurities that people were feeling in the department. People had picked "a safe, nurturing environment" as a value. Her team thought, at the time, that this was very typical for a fire department. Safety is very high on the agenda, but it wasn't just about physical safety. It was psychological safety, to speak your mind and have an opinion. The whole first set of values stemmed from the unrest, lack of teamwork, and negativism within the culture.

Years later, their values had shifted to being very outward focused on what they provided the citizens—their community—and how they provided service. Those things that were important to the community became part of the culture. Fire service personnel stopped looking internally at just themselves, and began to focus on values that centered on how to serve their community better. It took them a long time.

When the students returned to give their report on the new set of values, her team was stunned at the results.

The report was validating. The department had switched its focus. This wasn't easy; it took time and concentration. As far as being values-based, they were good at some things, and not so good at others. But Michos came to believe in the process as she watched her people change.

For example, one of their values was: "Be nice." There was an instance when she had to fire one of her firefighters for being perpetually late to work. The man she was firing said, "You're not being very nice." He was talking about the values. She said to him, "Someday you are going to realize this is the nicest thing that somebody could have done to you at this point in your life." It was a life lesson. Nothing else seemed to get across to him. He needed to come to work on time.

Michos' story of leadership, which led to cultural change over a long period of time, exhibits an unusual level of personal situation awareness and evolving confidence. Not all of her moments were in a flow state, but looking at how both she and her department transformed over time illustrates the connection between conscious flow-based decision making and leadership.

Time-Constrained Events

Emergency situations have a time component. The situation changes rapidly due to all sorts of variables, such as fire, chemical spills, rapidly changing health issues, volatile interpersonal relationships, and so on. These events require leaders to respond rapidly. There isn't time to evaluate multiple options. Kahneman's System 1 thinking has to kick in, but from a place of understanding the options. This is facilitated by training and experience.

For example, a firefighter Mayday requires strong autocratic leadership. In this case, the incident commander must maintain (a) radio discipline to determine location and situation, and (b) team integrity. When a firefighter is in trouble, his or her teammates' first impulse is to rush in to help him or her. It is up to the fire officer to contain the situation. These situations happen very fast in real time. Firefighters must get into a flow state instantaneously; be conscious and aware in each moment; make the right decisions; and later, detach and debrief to facilitate the betterment of process. Debriefing the incident upon immediate return to quarters is essential to "reinforce good practices and…identify any unacceptable performance."[73]

The next three sections are stories that illustrate these concepts. The first story is one every seasoned firefighter in America knows. It was originally told to me by the incident commander, who made the hard decision to stop searching for his lost firefighters. The second is the story that came about as a result of subsequent training developed based on the events in the first story. The third is the follow-up story to the second, illustrating the importance of follow through, debriefing, and analysis that has to happen for learning and prevention in future incidents.

Worcester Cold Storage Warehouse Fire

All of the stories I collected in my study contained elements of flow. However, the one that had 100 percent of all the characteristics of flow was the story of the Worcester, Massachusetts Cold Storage Warehouse fire that occurred on

[73] IAFCNFPA, 2006

December 3, 1999. It is also a perfect example of flow-based leadership. Retired District Fire Chief Michael O. McNamee related this story to me while I was sitting at his kitchen table in Worcester in 2010.

About the Worcester Fire Department

Worcester is the second largest city in New England. The Worcester Fire Department is the second largest fire department in New England. The Worcester Cold Storage Warehouse was an enormous building. The two main sections of the warehouse were built in 1908 and 1912. Another section, which created an L-wing off the rear of the building, was built decades later. The warehouse had six floors and no windows. The walls were 18 inches thick. There were only three stairwells. One of those stairwells only went to the second floor offices. Another stairwell went to the third floor by way of the rear loading dock. Only one very narrow stairwell down at the far left-hand side of the building went to all six floors, servicing the major area of the building. That was the only way out from the three upper floors. The stairs were made of black steel, like fire escape stairs with solid treads. The stairwell was so narrow that "when firefighters were passing each other, they really had to squeeze. One would be grinding against the wall; the other would be leaning back over the railing. That's how it was for six stories. Two turns per floor."

Incident Description

On December 9, 1999 a homeless couple who had been living in the warehouse accidently set a fire. Unbeknownst to responding firefighters, the couple had left the building. Two firefighters went to the roof of the building to ventilate it. They then entered the building from there to search for the couple. They searched the sixth floor, which was clear, and descended to the fifth floor. They had made their way to the part of the building most remote from the one stairwell, when things suddenly went bad. The black, acrid smoke filled the area, creating zero visibility in less than five seconds. They became disoriented and couldn't find their way out.

Eventually, they ran out of air. Four more firefighters were sent in to rescue them. They got lost in the building as well. In the meantime, the fire continued to burn hotter and hotter.

Mike McNamee was the incident commander on the B (or left) side of the building, where the stairwell was that went to all of the floors. He had firefighters queued up to continue the search for those lost in the building. They searched for about an hour and fifteen minutes on three separate floors before Chief McNamee made his decision to turn the effort from a rescue to a recovery. Each report that came down from the teams got worse and worse. The report that prompted Mike to make his decision to go defensive was delivered by Jimmy Pijus, "a very seasoned, well-respected lieutenant." Here is McNamee's account of that decision making process:

> "[Jimmy] put his butt on the second step. I'm in this narrow hallway at the base of the stairway. He took his mask off. He held his mask and he looked up at me. He was literally steaming. That's how hot he was. He said, 'Chief, I couldn't make it past the third floor.' His assignment was to go to the fourth floor. We were searching the third, the fourth, and the fifth.
>
> "That's what made me take a step back. I looked out into the hallway. There were a dozen

guys standing there. Many of them I'd known since they'd been on the job. I knew some of their wives. I knew some of their children. I just looked out at them and said, 'This has to stop. I just can't do this. I can't send them in there anymore.' But I didn't come out with the decision right then.

"I took that step back and I walked up to the doorway leading out to the open area, and that's when I said, 'That's it. That's it. We're done.' I got hit back with a whole lot of protest. When I made that one statement that we'd already lost six, it really hit them hard. It had a physiological effect on them. Their shoulders dropped; heads went down; their arms slumped, almost universally, right down the line of about a dozen firefighters. I said, 'Let's get ready to go outside and go into defensive mode, and see if we can keep this thing from going to all the other buildings around.'

"I had to stand in the doorway with my feet against the jambs and my hands like this [puts his hands up as if he were holding the doorframe]. I had to scream at them, because they were coming towards me.

"From that point on, I knew it was sending good after bad. All I was going to do was add to the casualties. It was very clear. It's one of the most distinguished moments of clarity I've ever had in my life. The decision was not muddled. It was not panicked.

"We were rotating teams of firefighters to go in. I actually stopped and I considered for probably a full minute before I said to the guys who were waiting to go up, 'That's it. No more. We're done.' They screamed at me. They were angry. They were *really* angry. They screamed. I yelled back. I said, 'You listen to me. We already lost six. We are not going to lose any more.' It was like somebody had collectively kicked every one of them in the stomach. Their shoulders slumped. Heads went down. It felt like failure: 'We didn't get the job done. We didn't do what we were supposed to do.' We're supposed to have a good outcome, especially when it comes to us."

Aftermath

McNamee and his crew were fairly sure where the missing firefighters were when they got into trouble: "The first two couldn't have been any further from that stairwell. They were at the furthermost point in that maze-like building."

The firefighters referred to the warehouse as an evil building. During one of the press briefings that Mike gave, he dubbed it "the building from hell," because:

"It just handed us our heads. It kicked our butts in a very, very solid way. We weren't used to that. We hadn't lost a firefighter in a violent line of duty death in thirty-seven years. We had had our heart attacks. We had our aneurisms, and a lot of serious injuries and burns, but we hadn't lost one in this way in all that time. It was always in the back of your mind that you had that possibility, but that incident brought it full-face front. From then on, everyone had a different attitude towards the job. It's kind of funny, because you see the people that were hired since then don't have that attitude. It's been interesting."

The fire department responded quickly to facilitate the recovery of the lost firefighters. The critical incident stress team was deployed that night. A tent city was set up, with dormitory tents and cafeteria tents. They searched around the clock for eight days in the New England winter for the men they lost. Because the sixth, fifth, fourth, and third floors of the building had all collapsed onto the second floor, they had to sift through the rubble by hand. McNamee knew what floors the men were on, but once the collapse occurred, he did not know where they would finally be.

> "The fire was a Friday night. It wasn't until the following Saturday night [over a week later] at eight o'clock when we found the last one, Paul Brotherton. He had six sons. The oldest was about eleven. Ironically, that firefighter's wife finally said, as she handed a bottle of Sam Adams to one of the firefighters, 'Here, you go. Put this up there and you will find him.' And, within about an hour-and-a-half, we found him. There were a lot of freaky things that happened.

> "Another freaky thing happened when we found Paul. The two walls of this huge brick warehouse that were still standing had no windows... Somebody said, 'Look!' High up on one of the two walls, at full height, a piece of asphalt-impregnated cork that insulated this cold storage warehouse ignited. It hadn't been doing anything the whole eight days, and all of a sudden, that thing up there ignited. We packaged Paul and got him all ready to take down. We had a ceremony. We had a ritual we went through for each guy. As soon as we handed him off the deck on the second floor, which remained intact, down to the people on the ladder to take him down—as soon as he reached the ground, somebody said, 'Hey, look!' We looked up, and the fire was out. It burned from the time we found him until the time we got him out of the building. We all just looked

at each other. I'm not making this up. This happened. Many, many people saw it. There were a few things like that that just gave us the willies."

McNamee's decision on the night of the fire resulted in the avoidance of further loss of life. But the experience in Worcester has impacted the fire service across the world. To date, I have yet to meet a firefighter who has not heard of the Worcester Cold Storage Warehouse Fire. The Worcester Fire Department has presented seminars all over the country using the lessons they learned. Mike was sure that these seminars saved lives, as evidenced in this story:

"What happened in Worcester rocked the fire service in the nation and Canada. We have done a lot of good since then. Some of us from the department have spoken all over the country, to go out with a lessons learned approach. We've done seminars on saving your own.

"Over six years, we trained over three thousand firefighters in twenty-nine states and three Canadian provinces. They come to Worcester every October and they get their eyes opened up, because we learned the hard way. We know—we've had feedback—we know that lives have been saved, not only because of what happened in Worcester, but because of what we, as Worcester firefighters, did with that. There was a core group of us that said, 'We've got to share this. We've got to let people know.'

"For example, another training chief and I did a presentation in Jersey City to about four hundred firefighters. We went through the whole incident. That was in December following the fire, a year later. The following February, two months after we were there, they had a fire with the identical type of cold storage warehouse, right at the mouth of the Holland Tunnel, called Mecca Trucking. The chief of Jersey City actually took us there to show us. We couldn't believe it. It was the same—paint color schemes, same era, probably designed by the same architect, because everything was so similar. When they pulled up, they got the same reports we did in our incident when we first got to the scene: There were homeless people living in the warehouse. They were ready to charge in. But, all of a sudden, they all stopped.

"The Battalion Chief from Jersey City called me that night and he said, 'Mike!' He was almost jumping up and down. I know the guy. He's a friend, and I could picture him. And he said, 'Mike, Mike, Mike, you wouldn't believe it!' He said, 'If it hadn't been for what happened in Worcester, we would have lost ten guys today, at least.' All of a sudden, all the Jersey City firefighters started looking at each other saying, 'Worcester. Shades of Worcester. Think Worcester.' And every one of them got out. They didn't get caught in there. They were all on ropes. They had to find their way out. They found homeless people in there, actually. They did rescue the two homeless, where, in our case, the two homeless had left.

"So we know a lot of good has come out of a very bad thing for us. That helps. That helps a lot. It has been an experience. Talk about your life-altering events!"

McNamee's own decision to continue working after the warehouse fire had far-reaching implications. He participated in seminars; he spoke to other departments; he had the opportunity to work with Worcester's own firefighters. He said, "I tried to work hard to make sure that we were doing everything we could to keep this from happening again. And I worked ten years after the fire. And I'm really glad that I did."

McNamee became Worcester's first full-time safety officer, which is a position in the Incident Command System, the standard method for managing incidents in the fire service. McNamee worked the day shift, but then got called back on incidents that happened when he was off. The Incident Command System requires that, at every incident, the incident commander must name a safety officer.[74] If he or she does not, then the incident commander must serve as both incident commander and safety officer. This is very hard, because they are two very separate roles. The incident commander must focus on operations, including strategies and tactics. The safety officer focuses on making sure everything is going correctly, the stability of the building—the integrity of the structure— making sure there is compliance with safety standards, and being aware of the individual actions of the firefighters.

> "Are we getting to be a little kamikaze? That's another thing firefighters tend to be, especially the young guys. You've got to really rein them back, and you get the dirty look. They just don't get it. When you have been around for a little while, you keep seeing a lot of things happening. Over the course of my eight years as safety chief, I know I kept a lot of guys from getting hurt on scenes."

McNamee received positive feedback over the years from his fellow firefighters in his own department. He spoke specifically about the firefighters in his immediate command that fateful night.

---

[74] Brunacini & Brunacini, 2004

"I could see a lot of fear in the eyes of those dozens of firefighters who were in line waiting to go up and I gave them their instructions. But they all went. Every single one of them that was standing there that night waiting to go up came to me at some point after—some took six months—and they thanked me. They didn't think so that night, but they told me it was absolutely the right thing to do."

Once, when he and one of the other chiefs spoke at the Fire Safety Officers' Conference in Florida a few years ago, the head safety chief for New York City and one of his battalion chiefs approached him:

"They said, 'It was a tough decision. You really did the right thing. Don't ever second guess yourself.' Then the battalion chief, who worked for the deputy chief in charge of the whole safety division for the New York Fire Department said to me, 'Hey, chief, you know how we would have handled that, if that was New York? We would have kept throwing guys at it until we lost twelve or fifteen.' And he said, 'My hat is off to you.'"

McNamee took a great deal of solace from this positive feedback. Within the department he and others encouraged this thinking. But even with this positive feedback, McNamee was situationally aware of his own state of being and took immediate steps to take care of himself.

"I went for a lot of help afterwards. There were many programs offered in systems stress and critical incident stress management. I spent a lot of time [working through this]. I have a wonderful family. I have two great daughters, who are my best friends, and a wonderful wife. About three months after the fire, I could see the dark clouds. I thought I was alright. 'I'm okay. I'm okay. I'm okay.' You can see the dark clouds coming and you start to feel a downward pull. I just said, 'I'm not letting this happen.'

"All of my memorabilia is in a big box up in my loft. I put it in there and I closed it. I put it away. It's something that is ten years behind now, but it is right with me [points next to the space next to the right side of his body]. You move forward, but you don't get past it. But you have to keep moving forward. I don't like the alternative."

Tie-In to Leadership

The Worcester Cold Storage Warehouse fire is an example of two approaches to leadership. There were two firehouses involved in the incident. Chief McNamee's station—the central station—responded openly, to the public and each other. The other house went into bunker mode, trying to hide what happened.

Sometimes one has to make decisions that do not fit into the stated goals of safety and the desire for everyone to go home at the end of the day. His moment of decision "was one of the clearest moments of my life. I was definitely in the flow."

"We didn't do anything wrong that night. We fought that fire the way we fought a thousand others, and the building just beat us. The fire was a Friday night. Sunday morning, the chief of the department asked me to do the press briefing. There were twenty microphones, eighty reporters, satellite trucks all over the place. This was a huge incident. I said, '[Chief,] how do you want me to handle this?' He said, 'Tell them what happened.' I said, 'Thank you.' We were an open book right from the beginning. This attitude really helped us get through this.

"Two of the guys that died worked at the station where I worked. The other four who died worked out of our headquarters station on the same shift. The guys at the central station, where I worked, talked. We were open about it. We just kept putting it out there, back and forth. Somebody would say something and we purged. We just unloaded and unloaded.

"The other house made an actual verbal pact with each other not to talk to anybody outside their house. They built a cocoon around themselves. You could feel the anger and the negativity in that group. The entire department called them a cancer on the department because of the way they handled it. They also thought they had the right to tell others how they're supposed to handle their grief. You can't do that. Everybody does it in their own way.

"Last fall [2009], the first time in ten years, they actually sat down with a member of the press and told their side of the story, which was no different from ours. It was just that they had been angry about it. They didn't get past that anger stage. Even people in that shift in that house would come to me and said, 'You know, you did everything right that night.' And I know I did. That's one of the reasons I can live with myself. If I had made some bad calls that night, I wouldn't have bounced back. What we did is what we do. Most of the guys in that house, they told me, 'It's not against you.' But they had this anger and they didn't know where to put it. So they put it out on everybody that crossed their path.

"This did not impact their ability to fight fire. Several of them got promoted to lieutenant and were shipped out. But as soon as there was an opening back in that house, on that shift, they transferred back. It was almost like a co-dependence that they had with each other. Everybody else was saying, 'You know, it wasn't just your loss. This was everybody's loss. We all felt this.' This isn't solely owned by this group of fifteen people here. It was very interesting what happened afterwards.

"Our house was all open. We talked and we talked, and we cried, and we talked and we cried."

Mike McNamee exhibited flow-based leadership in every aspect of this story. He was able to switch from a collaborative leadership style to an autocratic leadership style while maintaining the trust of his people. Even though they wanted to keep searching for the missing men, they respected his decision. His situational awareness was spot on, not only during the incident, but also during the search, investigation, and recognition that lessons learned needed to be shared with other departments. Finally, and probably most importantly, he was aware of the impact the incident had on his own well-being, prompting him to put into place appropriate coping mechanisms.

Kyle Wilson Story

This story was the impetus for my doctoral work. It was told to me by my brother-in-law, Steve Strawderman, retired Battalion Chief of Prince William County, Virginia, Department of Fire and Rescue (PWCDFR). It is the story of a line of duty death that happened on his watch. On April 16, 2007, Technician 1

Kyle R. Wilson, a firefighter in service with the PWCDFR, lost his life in the line of duty. Steve was one of the battalion chiefs assigned to that fire. A few months prior to this incident, Steve viewed the training video of the classes conducted by the Worcester Fire Department.

At 6 a.m. on April 16, 2007, a call came into PWCDFR. It was a three-alarm house fire. By the time Steve arrived at the scene, firefighters were already engaged. An assumption had been made that there were people still in the house. As it turned out, everyone had managed to get out. The incident commander, not knowing this, sent in Kyle and his partner to evacuate the building. The house was burning very fast. Later analysis showed that the wind came through the back of the house and up the stairs from the basement, fueling the fire. The building collapsed between Kyle and his partner, trapping Kyle.

PWCDFR had just adopted a new state-of-the-art Motorola communication system that failed in the critical moments of this incident due to heavy water being put on the burning house. However, when Kyle became trapped, his fellow firefighters heard his call for help (Mayday). Their first instinct was to run into the building to save him. Steve was no exception, but all the training kicked in before he could. In that very chaotic moment—in the midst of his flow state—Steve stopped, literally stood in the doorway to the burning house, held up his arms in the same fashion Mike McNamee did in the Worcester incident, and said, "No more." He told me he had to physically keep the other firefighters from rushing into the house. He was able to adopt the necessary command presence to effectively make the right call in that chaotic moment, but this effectiveness was facilitated by the respect and trust the other firefighters had for him.

That day, PWCDFR and the world lost Kyle, but because of Steve's ability to consciously, creatively suspend his instinctive urge to act, he made the right decision and acted in a way that avoided further loss of life, immeasurably altering the lives of those firefighters, their families, and their communities.

Steve's action has resulted in far-reaching changes. MSA, one of the manufacturers of the air packs the firefighters wear, shut down its plant of 450 workers to hear Kyle's story and has since modified its air packs, with improvements recommended by the fire service as a direct result of the conditions in Kyle's death. Motorola also worked with PWCDFR regarding the multiple radio failures during this incident.[75] In addition, every year since Kyle's death, there has been a 10K walk in Kyle's name to benefit the Kyle Wilson Memorial Scholarship Fund, set up "to benefit students who wish to attend the George Mason University Athletic Training Program."[76]

Michos' Role in Wilson LODD

Retired PWCDFR Fire Chief Mary Beth Michos told me her follow-up story involving the aftermath of Kyle Wilson's line of duty death (LODD). As Chief of the department, she was responsible for making all the decisions to get 300 people through the aftermath of that incident. When she was en route to the scene, one of her firefighters radioed that a firefighter was lost, and then radioed again when they found him. She remembered asking over the radio, "How is he?" The firefighter replied, "Not good." She knew then that Kyle was dead.

---

[75] Strawderman, interview, 2009

[76] WDCW/DC50TV, 2010

She told me she thought, "I am the chief of the department. What do I need to do in this role?" The answer was clear: She had to take care of the people.

The processes were in place for the investigation of the fire incident, but she knew that she needed to help her people get through this loss. She learned this lesson from another line of duty death experience in 1976, when she was "only a captain," but was the head of EMS. She lost one of her paramedics while he was on duty. He was killed in an accident in the medic unit.

> "It was so different back then. I didn't have much control over things and how things were handled. I was the only woman in the department. I was young. I was still in my twenties when [the paramedic] died. I took care of everything that had to be handled as far as the funeral, and I wouldn't let anyone see me cry. I thought, 'I can't let them see me cry. They'll say I'm a weak woman.'"

Every year after the paramedic's death, her department held an anniversary memorial. On the 10th anniversary:

> "I was at the gravesite with everybody, and I was crying. One of the paramedics…was crying. We were holding each other, and he said, 'You know, I needed to cry when [the paramedic] died, but you didn't cry, and I, as a man, couldn't cry, because you, as a woman, weren't crying.' I thought, 'What a disservice I did.' But I didn't know any better.
>
> "When Kyle Wilson [the firefighter in more recent line of duty death] died, I kept telling people you have to show your emotions. You have to give others permission by showing your own emotions. So, I cried when the situation

was appropriate, even in public and with others after Kyle died."

She understood, from this past experience, that an incident that results in a line of duty death can either tear a department apart, or bring it closer together. Ultimately, she was able to guide PWCDFR in a way that brought everyone together.

She told me that she wasn't sure if she was consciously aware of her decisions during this time. However, she was able to quickly prioritize what she had to do. She knew that the first people she and her chief officers had to take care of were Kyle's family and the crew that was involved in the incident. She understood that she couldn't do this all by herself. She relied heavily on administrative support to carry on the work in the office, and on her assistant chiefs because, in her words, "I'm only one person."

She and the assistant chiefs worked to develop a plan that could be implemented immediately. For three or four days, until the funeral, they didn't even go to their offices. They spent all their time with the people who had been impacted. They visited with every shift in every station. Their goal was to let the entire department know that they were in this together—to answer questions, and to grieve with them.

Part of their plan was to prepare for the funeral and for the investigation. Michos wanted to make sure that something positive came out of Kyle's death by establishing the basics for what was going to happen in years to come as a result of Kyle's death.

Michos' goal-oriented approach to leadership was transformational and service-oriented. All the elements of flow are contained in her story, but what stands out most is her selflessness and attention to the task at hand while keeping the needs of her people and community in the forefront.

Flow-Based Leadership Empowers Others

As we have seen in these stories, flow-based leadership is amorphous. It might be autocratic one minute, and collaborative or transformative the next. When executed with grace, humility, courage, and an outward focus, it instills trust and respect in followers, and empowers followers to be leaders themselves by example. This way of being demonstrates and encourages ethical character.[77]

Helen Graham's commitment to the establishment of a national policy on how firefighters are treated when they receive burns while fighting wildland fires has resulted in the empowerment of firefighters in the field. In one instance, when a firefighter received severe burns to his foot, the captain of his hotshot crew asked Graham if they needed to follow the new protocol, which was to transfer the injured firefighter from the rural hospital to an approved regional burn center. Graham said, "Yes, you do."

> "The captain knows me and my role. He understood what I meant when I told him that... He told me later that my instructions changed everything in his head about how we were going to operate. We have our policy that was based on our slides, and we're not going to let this happen again.
>
> "When he heard me say that to him on the phone, he felt empowered. He also felt obligated. He felt like he knew what he needed to do, but it changed his thought process."

---

[77] Kolditz, 2007

Empowering others to make the appropriate decisions instills confidence and a sense of control, which is essential to operating in flow.

Conclusion

A strict command-and-control mindset no longer works in today's world. Flow-based leadership, by definition, involves using the appropriate leadership style for the situation. Knowing what type of leadership to use depends on training; knowing when to use that type of leadership is facilitated by experience.

Flow is not time-bound. It can occur in rapidly emergent situations, but it can also occur over time. Both the Kyle Wilson story and the Worcester story involved flow-based leadership experiences that had both short-term and long-term aspects. Both incidents have had huge impacts on the fire service and beyond. Even though they occurred many years ago, these stories are still discussed and debated.

There is a program in Georgia called AXIOMS of Leadership. It is a program that focuses on leadership, and consists of both classroom time and team problem solving using props. The props are all based on incidents that occurred in either the fire service or the military. There is one instructor per team. The instructor explains the rules for the prop and describes the goal or mission for that prop. The team has five minutes to pick a leader and decide on an approach to completing the mission. They have 55 minutes to complete the mission. At the end of the time period, the instructor debriefs the team about what worked, what didn't work, whether they changed the plan, and how they worked together. At the close of the debrief, the instructor tells the story of the prop.

One of the props is called the Worcester Six. I've attended five of these training sessions (I was an actual participant in January 2014). I have begun to make it a point to be at the Worcester Six prop during each debrief. The discussion often goes something like this: "That must have been the hardest decision the Chief [Mike MacNamee] had to make. I can't imagine making that decision." It is natural that we think this way. I, too, struggle to imagine that it was otherwise. And, yet, I sat at Mike's kitchen table and heard him say,

> "From that point on, I knew it was sending good after bad. All I was going to do was add to the casualties. It was very clear. It's one of the most distinguished moments of clarity I've ever had in my life. The decision was not muddled. It was not panicked."

When I tell the AXIOMS students what Mike said about the decision he made, I see their faces change. They change how they think about how hard it would be to make a life and death decision. Because Mike was willing to share this moment with me, he has been able to affect the decisions of others far beyond his immediate reach and offer a level of empowerment and self-forgiveness to those who hear his story.

5 Georgia Smoke Diver Model

"I will never consider defeat, and I will remove from my vocabulary such words as quit, cannot, unable, impossible, failure, and retreat, for these are the words of fools and cowards."

—The Georgia Smoke Diver Creed

I learned about the Georgia Smoke Diver (GSD) program while I was doing my doctoral research. I published my dissertation in November 2011, and sent a copy to all my participants. David Rhodes had been a participant in my study. When he received my dissertation, he invited me to observe the November 2011 class. What began as a simple observation turned into a full-blown ethnography of this amazing group of firefighters.

The fire service has thousands of training programs. There are even many state run Smoke Diver programs. Most of these programs are three or four days long, and are run by state fire academies. The Georgia Smoke Diver program, which is for structural firefighters, runs for seven days and is one of the most advanced, high-intensity training programs in the fire service. In addition, while it is sanctioned by the Georgia Fire Academy, it is its own stand-alone entity.

The Georgia Smoke Diver program has been in existence since 1978. Cortez Lawrence (GSD #1) designed the original course based on a combination of the European model of fire training and the Florida Smoke Diver program.[78]

In March 2016, the GSD program graduated its 51st class and its 948th Georgia Smoke Diver. Classes are taught in November and March of each year at either the Georgia Public Safety Training Center in Forsyth, Georgia, or the Dalton Fire Department Training Center in Dalton, Georgia. On average, classes begin with between 35 and 40 candidates, and graduate about half of those who begin the class.

When I arrived for my first observation, I was amazed by the number of instructors. The ratio of instructor to student was two to one at the beginning of the week, and had risen to three to one by the end. The instructors were all wearing khaki pants, black t-shirts, and black ball caps with numbers emblazoned on them. What struck me most about this scene was the fact that I could not distinguish rank. Fire chiefs, battalion chiefs, captains, lieutenants, and regular firefighters all wear the same uniform. The only person who wears a distinguishing piece of clothing is the commanding officer (also known as Smoke Daddy); the gold braid on his ball cap makes him easy to spot on the training ground.

The GSD instructors volunteer their time to teach, often using precious vacation time away from their families. They receive no monetary compensation. Their reward is in the doing, in the

---

[78] Georgia Smoke Diver, 2016

camaraderie, and the knowledge that they are helping other firefighters be safer in their jobs.

In addition to furthering the skills of firefighters to keep them safe in critical incidents, the class focuses on training leaders, thereby building an organization of peer leaders. Leadership in the GSD program is based on the concepts of servant leadership. The philosophy of giving back and paying it forward permeates every aspect of the class, creating the next generation of instructor leaders and ensuring the sustainability of the program.

Internally, the group refers to itself as an elite group, but their outward focus is on service. Speeches by various instructors throughout the week stress to candidates that they are no better than anyone else. Instructors encourage candidates to go back to their departments and share what they have learned. They are emboldened to set the example for mental and physical preparedness and to give their all in service to their departments, families, and communities, in and out of uniform.

Leadership Structure

The structure of the GSD organization is very flat. The Board of Elders makes the strategic decisions for the organization. They solicit and encourage continuous input from the membership. There is a nomination and election process used to fill vacancies on the Board of Elders.

In 2013, the Board of Elders decided to add the level of deacon in recognition of longtime members of the organization who have demonstrated commitment to the program.

Everyone who has completed the class is a lead instructor, instructor, or intern instructor. Instructors continue to learn and must complete specific instructor training with each succeeding class. Intern instructors shadow instructors and lead instructors, and participate in instruction with greater and greater responsibilities with each class they attend.

Smoke Daddy Designation

The term Smoke Daddy refers to the leader of the Georgia Smoke Diver program. GSD members, those who have completed the class, elect the Smoke Daddy. There have only been five members selected to serve as Smoke Daddy since the program's inception:

- Smoke Daddy #1: Cortez Lawrence, GSD #1, 1978–1981 (Currently with U.S. Department of Homeland Security.)
- Smoke Daddy #2: Rob Fowler, GSD #10, 1981–1983 (retired as the fire chief of the LaGrange, Georgia Fire Department.)
- Smoke Daddy #3: John McLaughlin, GSD #9, 1983–1984 (retired as chief of operations for the Cobb County, Georgia, Fire Department.)
- Smoke Daddy #4: Scott Millsap, GSD #25, 1985–1994 (retired as training captain from the City of Dalton Fire Department. Died September 23, 2002.)
- Smoke Daddy #5: David Rhodes, GSD #339, 1995–present (Currently serving as battalion chief for the City of Atlanta Fire Rescue Department.)

Smoke Daddy provides opportunities for instructors to share themselves intellectually and spiritually. He encourages instructors to spread their individual passion like seeds in the garden. Instructors have the freedom to innovate and revise methods, procedures, and motivation. This fosters a sense of belonging and contribution. Rhodes says that this is the "life of the program." In the GSD program, you won't ever hear anyone say, "That's not my job."

Course Content

Firefighters have to function in high stress, emergent situations. Every incident is different. Muscle memory is critical in these situations. According to Klein's recognition-primed decision making concepts, when we are in stressful situations, we make decisions based on previous similar experiences and training, and use solutions that worked in those situations.[79] Drilling over and over on both basic and not-so-basic activities frees the mind to deal with the anomalies that occur in all emergent activities.[80]

Instructors teach the drills incrementally so that they instill muscle memory. Drills begin with the basics, the mechanics of how a task is done, in an open, stress-free environment. Later during the week, students must complete the same drills in a simulated fireground scenario with the addition of smoke, fire, zero visibility, running water, and loud noises.

Recent research shows that "emotion and vividness influence fluency, availability, and judgments of probability."[81] Drills are often based on past incidents in which firefighters lost their lives in the line of duty. This practice attaches an emotional

[79] Klein, 1999

[80] Kahneman, 2011

[81] *Ibid*

component and meaning to the drill that solidifies the learning. Knowing *why* reinforces the commitment to excellence.

It is human nature to underweight rare events. In other words, we tend to believe that if it has never happened or rarely happens, it won't happen on our watch. This can result in neglect and complacency. Even firefighters, who see the unusual and unexpected every day, can be subject to this line of thinking. Remember, Mike McNamee said that Worcester hadn't lost a firefighter in over 30 years. *They didn't think it could happen to them.* Training for "choice from experience" helps combat the tendency to underweight potentially life-threatening, unexpected scenarios.[82]

One of the biggest contributors to bad decision making in emergent situations is fatigue.[83] In an effort to simulate high stress incidents, the class begins every day with high intensity physical training (PT) in full gear. Following PT, students complete a strenuous obstacle course, which includes a hoisting exercise and tire pull, among other strength-based tasks. This is followed by a three-mile run. This physical activity is not for the purpose of tearing down candidates, but for making them tired at the beginning of the day. Their ability to think and decide is then compromised. Although there is only anecdotal evidence, the leaders of the GSD program believe this training regimen provides seven years of decision making experience in seven days.

Firefighters who return to the class after becoming a Smoke Diver also participate in training. Every level of instructor is

---

[82] Kahneman, 2011

[83] Glick-Smith, 2011

always in training. Each instructor must complete task books for each level of training.

Spreading the Good Word

The GSD program is not just for Georgia firefighters. There are quite a few out-of-state members. However, this wasn't always the case. Only recently has the program allowed firefighters from outside of Georgia into the class. This policy changed when David Rhodes was hired to manage the logistics at the Fire Department Instructors' Conference (FDIC) in Indianapolis every year. As time went on, other Georgia Smoke Divers began to assist in the logistics effort. They would wear their GSD t-shirts while working at FDIC. This got the attention of Captain Matt Stewart, of the Wayne Township, Indiana, Fire Department, who was assigned to be the local logistics connection.

Indiana Smoke Diver Program

Stewart became friends with the Georgia Smoke Divers while working with them at FDIC. He was impressed with their work ethic and their strong sense of community. Stewart asked Rhodes about the program. Rhodes told him this was a Georgia program that didn't allow out-of-state students. However, Rhodes worked out an arrangement with the Georgia Fire Academy to accommodate out-of-state students who were willing to pay tuition. Pete Woodall (GSD #661) from Ohio and Matt Stewart (GSD #662, Indiana Smoke Diver (ISD) #1, and ISD Smoke Daddy) were the first and second out-of-state firefighters to go through the GSD program.

Indiana didn't have advanced firefighter or survival training. Matt began to promote the Georgia Smoke Diver program in his department. As of this writing, over 15 members of his department have successfully completed the GSD program. These firefighters wanted to start their own Smoke Diver program. They were able to convince the Indiana Department of Homeland Security Division of Fire Training to sanction their new program by offering a certificate of completion to those who finished it.

The Indiana Smoke Diver program, modeled after the GSD program, began in the fall of 2013. Members of the GSD program went to Indiana to help with that first class. They also supported them with start-up funds and the services of their webmaster, Chris Cook (GSD #383).

The GSD program ensured the success of the ISD program by providing them with a tried and true framework, which is thoroughly documented. In addition, all of the ISD instructors in that first class were also Georgia Smoke Divers. The first class of ISD was almost identical to the GSD program. To date, ISD has had three training classes and now has 29 Indiana Smoke Divers.

Oklahoma Smoke Diver Program

In September of 2013, firefighters from Edmond, Oklahoma, attended a conference in Rogers, Arkansas, where David Rhodes was speaking. They noticed the GSD rocker on Rhodes' slides and asked him about the program. They went home and researched the GSD program. They presented the idea of going through the GSD training to their department. Five Oklahoma firefighters completed the GSD program in March 2014. As of March 2016, there are seven Oklahoma Smoke Divers.

The Oklahoma Smoke Divers are now in the planning stages for creating their own program. The GSD Elders are working with them to get their infrastructure and procedures in place so that they are ready to launch when they have reached a critical mass of Smoke Diver Instructors for their program. Lindall Wood (GSD #882 and OSD #2), with the support of a very receptive fire service organization in Edmond and the help of the GSD program, wants to create a training program that will prepare Oklahoma firefighters to be the best for the citizens they serve.

Model for Creating Flow-Based Organizations

The Georgia Smoke Diver program represents a model of service and community, as shown in Figure 7: Flow-based Leadership Manifesto, that can be duplicated successfully in other public service organizations. GSD is a group of equals, leaders committed to service.

How the GSD program manages to sustain itself from year to year has to do with member commitment to excellence and the mission of the program: to make firefighters better. After studying them for the past five years, I have identified very specific characteristics that facilitate their longevity, passion, and dedication to their profession. The following characteristics of the GSD program form a framework for flow-based leadership:

- Lead by example.
- Communicate clearly.
- Commit to a stable infrastructure.

- Bind the group by cultivating trust.
- Honor individual creativity for innovation.
- Use positive motivation techniques.
- Facilitate team flow.

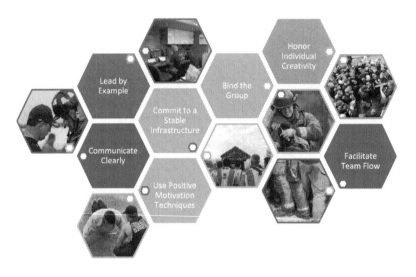

Figure 7: Flow-based Leadership Manifesto

To duplicate this framework, there has to be commitment on the part of leadership at both departmental and governmental levels. The flow-based leadership framework will not work in departments where leaders make fear-based decisions, decisions that hurt others, or decisions that focus on power. Decisions must be based on love and respect for the job, the professional community, and the community served.

While there is a fireground need for hierarchy in command structure, treating all members of the team with equal respect and honor can result in a paradigm shift that recognizes the team as a group of equals—leaders committed to service.

Conclusion

The Georgia Smoke Diver program is, in my experience, an anomaly in organizational development practices. I have heard organizational leaders in the business world, the not-for-profit realm, and the public service sector often put forward elements of this model. However, leaders pick and choose those elements that suit their own needs, which may be related to financial gain, ego boosts, or power grabs. What seems to be missing is the sense of purpose, a sense of service toward the customer or the public, and honor and respect toward the people actually doing the work of the organization.

The GSD program is successful and has demonstrated longevity through its leaders' commitment to purpose, infrastructure, inclusion, camaraderie, service, creativity, and innovation. All these elements have to be in place to sustain an organization over time. The following chapter explores this framework in detail.

6 Creating Flow-based Organizations

"Change-making happens when people fall in love with a different version of the future."

—Seth Godin

A flow-based organization is one that recognizes that its people are the key to its success. Leadership operates in flow, while facilitating flow for every individual in the organization. It is not necessarily a nirvana with little or no conflict. However, it is an organization that manages its conflict well, while honoring all points of view and the diversity that enables creativity and innovation. Communication is open, and people listen to one another with respect in order to facilitate dialogue. All ideas matter, even if not all can be implemented.

Building an enterprise architecture to support this requires careful, mindful design across all functional, operational, and support areas of the organization. Being such a leader and enterprise architect requires self-knowledge coupled with a selfless, compassionate. and empathetic mindset. Being a flow-based leader means that you make the effort to learn who your employees are at their core, so that you can enable them to be successful. People are happier and more productive when they feel they are successfully contributing. There is no one-size-fits-all solution to this. For example, it is incorrect to think that every worker can only work for eight hours on a specific task. This is early 20th century, Adam Smith thinking. If a person is in flow, he or she can and will work until the task is complete: not because they have to, but because they *want* to. They enjoy the experience of getting it done.

The more people work in flow, the more they seek out opportunities to work in flow. They learn their own personal triggers of flow. They also understand they often need to do non-flow tasks in preparation to be in flow. Over time, however, these tasks can also become flow states because of their connection to moving into flow.

For example, in the fire service, firefighters know they need to stay physically strong to do their jobs. While an individual firefighter may not particularly enjoy physical training, he or she does PT every day in spite of the lack of enjoyment. He or she knows that is what will help facilitate success on the fireground. Over time, as the feeling of being strong and in touch with his or her body increases well-being, PT may actually trigger flow for that firefighter.

Flow tends to come and go within individuals, teams, and organizations. Empirical evidence over the last 20 years of organizational studies shows that communicating a purpose, demonstrating trust, encouraging and facilitating mastery, promoting self-management and self-directed processes, and encouraging worker autonomy are the most effective ways to motivate workers. If you pay people a living wage, these intrinsic rewards are much more effective than monetary awards.[84]

This chapter contains a framework, based on my study of the Georgia Smoke Diver (GSD) program, for establishing flow-based organizations. Authentically implementing and maintaining these components will enable your organization to grow and thrive even beyond your own time of service.

Lead by Example

A flow-based organization enables all of its members—leaders and followers—to be in flow as much as possible. While this is best driven and demonstrated by the highest leaders in the organization, each individual has the ability to implement flow-based decision making using the components described in this chapter. You do this by:

- Demonstrating your own commitment and ability to live and work in flow;
- Communicating your vision, goals, decisions, observations, and ideas and giving others the opportunity to communicate the same from their perspective;
- Mindfully providing the appropriate infrastructure and systems that support and provide feedback to your people (rather than get in the way of their ability to operate);
- Cultivating trust and a sense of belonging;

---

[84] Pink, 2009

- Honoring individual creativity;
- Using positive motivation techniques; and
- Learning what brings your people joy, so that you can provide them with training and opportunities to be in that space.

Using these concepts, GSD has cultivated an organization of leaders. Georgia Smoke Divers take responsibility for their individual actions, and are mindful of the actions of the organization. By doing so, they have managed to build an "evergreen" organization that perpetuates itself through grace, determination, grit, and commitment, along with love and caring for themselves, their fellow firefighters, their individual departments, and the communities they serve. Their reputation is solid throughout Georgia, and indeed, they are becoming known around the world through the leadership of Chief Elders Smoke Daddy David Rhodes and Operations Chief Brent Hullender.

Leadership Styles and Conflict Management

In the fire service, chief officers must adhere to ethical practices, because they are always being watched by the firefighters who report to them, the municipal bodies to whom they report, and the public for whom they serve. They must be able to address issues without hesitation using good, ethical judgment. In addressing ethical dilemmas, the chief officer must consciously recognize and define the situation, objectively identify the facts, list all the options, compare each option to established criteria, select the best option, double check the decision, and take action.[85]

However, every firefighter must take responsibility for his or her decisions and actions. On the fireground, everyone has a job to do. This requires self-leadership and responsibility; good communication skills, including the ability to remain calm in the face of danger; and the ability to put aside any team conflicts or house-related drama. Otherwise, team flow can't happen.

In the GSD program, leadership styles are as varied as the people who participate in the organization. There is a feeling of trust and respect among the instructors, regardless of leadership style or personality.

This doesn't mean there aren't conflicts. Conflicts indeed occur. However, they are managed appropriately. The Smoke Divers talk to each other. They know and honor each other's similarities and differences, because they have all completed what they know is the most rigorous training in the fire service. When conflicts are between two or three Smoke Divers, they work it out among themselves. Teams handle their internal issues quickly within the team. GSD leadership addresses larger conflicts when they occur. Sometimes this happens in the command office; in more severe situations, Smoke Daddy stops the training and pulls all of the instructors into the base room of the training tower. Guests are not allowed into this meeting. The issue is discussed and resolved quickly. This collaborative style of conflict management incorporates forgiveness as well as agreement. After a decision is reached, there is no further discussion of the issue; the decision reached is final. Instructors

---

[85] Stowell, 2004

go back to their jobs. To an outsider, it appears as if nothing ever happened.

On Being a Leader of Equals

David Rhodes believes he is a leader of equals, setting the tone for both students and instructors. He demonstrates this through his actions, attitude, and words. He gives his time and heart to the GSD program and to the profession. He is a constant contributor to the profession's knowledge base through his collaboration with Underwriters Laboratories' Firefighters Safety Research Institute which conducts fire behavior and fire suppression research, as well as through his writing and speaking. He works at the international level to promote fire service knowledge sharing among nations and cultures. He exhibits selfless, outward-facing compassion, love, and commitment. The people who know him are inspired to follow his lead.

We all have the opportunity to lead from time to time. In my experience and observation, there are fundamentally two types of leaders: (1) those who seek to control others, and (2) those who lead by example, with the intent of enabling others to operate from the best part of themselves.

When leaders seek to control others, they quickly find that those they lead will do only the bare minimum amount of work to get the job done. Followers stifle their own individuality and creativity, and turn off their critical thinking skills. They know the act of thinking critically or creatively will be perceived by the leader as an affront to his or her authority. Often, after giving what he or she perceives as clear instruction, the leader subsequently sabotages his or her own team in an effort to cover bad decisions or to elevate his or her image in the eyes of those to whom he or she reports. This type of leader is focused solely on himself or herself. He or she uses fear and intimidation as a means of control. This has the effect of destroying morale and the possibility of flow in any form from occurring.

People who seek to honor and respect those they lead find that people strive to do their best for themselves and their team. The leader sets and demonstrates the commitment to the vision. Creativity and critical thinking permeates everything the team does. This results in better service, less conflict, and a higher sense of well-being at both individual and organizational levels.

It doesn't matter if an individual is on the lowest rung of the organizational ladder. He or she can exhibit leadership through behavior, attitude, and effective communication. If something needs to be done, he or she can accept responsibility for making it happen. Lack of position is not a factor in the decision to take charge of the situation. In a healthy environment, leadership encourages this behavior. An organization of leaders operating together with a common vision is a powerful, awesome sight. The organization moves as one—able to change quickly and adjust to situations as they emerge.[86]

Taking Personal Responsibility

Flow-based leadership requires that the individual take responsibility for his or her own feelings, decisions, and actions. This requires a high level of self-awareness.

---

[86] Conversation with Barry Stevens, GSD #341, Firefighter/EMT, Coweta County, GA, Fire Department

Multiple Smoke Divers have told me stories about their journeys to excellence. Their drive to be the best they can be in all aspects of their lives is one of the things that binds them together. While all the stories are different, and quite powerful, the one common element among them is that the storytellers take personal responsibility for their own actions and continued education.

GSD Class #49 graduated its 900th Smoke Diver: Lt. Kevin Lolley of the Panama City Fire Department. It was his fifth attempt at completing the program. Because Lolley is from Florida, he had to pay tuition to attend the GSD training. He was bound and determined to become a Georgia Smoke Diver.

Two years before his last attempt, he decided to hire Dr. Ed Naggiar to help prepare him for the class. Naggiar is a former Navy Seal, and holds a Ph.D. in Industrial/Organizational Psychology. His area of expertise is performance under stress in extreme conditions. He founded an organization called Human Performance Consulting, LLC, to "improve the lives of thousands of individuals through resilience-based programs that are unmatched in the industry, by combining college level instruction with practical exercises and challenges taken from SEAL and High Risk Professional Experiences."[87]

With Naggiar's coaching, Lolley learned to focus his mind. One of the exercises Naggiar had Lolley do was to hold a plank position in full gear for ten minutes, merely by introducing powerful imagery to the exercise. Naggiar impressed upon Lolley that getting through the class was as much mental as physical. Naggiar also encouraged Lolley to step up and volunteer to be team leader in the GSD class. Lolley became one

---

[87] Human Performance Consulting, LLC, 2016

of the few team leaders to ever hold that position for the entire week of class. In Lolley's words:

> "Ed not only helped train me to a point to be able to complete [the class] but to a high enough level to feel comfortable and confident in taking on the class leader role on the first day. I made it through the entire week and was able to keep the position of class leader for the entire class— not a common occurrence.
>
> "I don't say this because I want you to be impressed with the personal accomplishment of being class leader, but so that you understand how well I was trained by Ed—not only physically, but mentally. See, he told me to take the class leader position; he knew I was ready for that kind of leadership responsibility, and that is the kind of training and leadership that Ed offers. He believed in me, and he committed to making me a fireman, a leader, a better man. That's what he does. I continue to train with Ed today!"

Lolley took responsibility for his own preparation to reach what he considered a worthy milestone. The lessons he learned from this experience have positively impacted his entire life.[88]

Honoring Those Who Came Before

Scott Millsap was voted in as Smoke Daddy in 1985. Millsap's number, 25, is on the side of the ball caps of many Smoke Divers in the GSD program. Of all the members of the GSD association, Scott Millsap looms largest. He was a firefighter and training captain in the City of Dalton, Georgia Fire

---

[88] Conversation with Lt. Kevin Lolley, GSD #900, Panama City, FL, Fire Department

Department. He served as Smoke Daddy of the GSD program until 1994.

Millsap was a charismatic leader and a powerful speaker. Those who knew him loved him and speak of him as the ultimate servant leader. His term of endearment for students was to call them COD. Some say this stands for candidate of distinction; others say it stands for courage, obligation, diligence. Leaders in the GSD program still refer to students and each other as COD.

In 1995, changes in the Georgia Fire Academy policies caused a rift between the GSD leadership and the Academy. However, Millsap believed in the GSD program. With a small group of instructors, he came up with a plan for delivering the class independently, without being sanctioned by the Georgia Fire Academy. His plan included securing a copyright on the Georgia Smoke Diver logo and program.

On September 23, 2002, Millsap died of cancer, but he left the GSD program to Brent Hullender (GSD # 593 and captain in the City of Atlanta Fire Rescue Department) with a charge to carry on the tradition. Hullender continues to serve as chief elder and operations chief for the program. Hullender assembled a Board of Elders to be the stewards of the program. Millsap's vision, passion, and commitment are alive in the GSD program. His story is told again and again, which reinforces the legacy he left.

Millsap set the example of quiet, confident, servant leadership for the program. The people who complete the training are both self-assured and humble, which are by-products of feeling confident.

Communicate

Millsap was a master communicator. GSD leaders often play the video of one of the last speeches he gave, which expresses his thoughts about what it means to lead. This serves to communicate Millsap's vision for the program, even though he is no longer around to implement it. His vision is sound, outward facing, and something that resonates in those who hear it.

Communication is the master key to successful, effective leadership. Communication permeates every aspect of leadership, whether it involves communicating with those who report to you, communicating with peers, or communicating with those to whom you report. Communication can be verbal or non-verbal; it can be face to face, or it can happen across communication systems. Communication is how we convey information from one person to another. For example, we use it to praise, show respect, reprimand, give instructions, show love, and convey intention.

How information is communicated can depend on many factors. Communication in the station house is different than communication on the training ground, which is different from that on the fireground in an emergent incident. The infrastructure that supports communication varies as well.

The most important of all organizational communication is the articulation of the mission and the vision. This drives how people respond in emerging incidents. However, each person should be aware of how he or she is feeling in the moment, striving for a level of peace within through positive self-talk and connection with his or her spiritual self. This practice helps one maintain a feeling of calm in the face of rapidly emergent situations. Finally, each person must take responsibility for communication within the team, and within the organization. This facilitates organizational success.

Communicate the Mission and the Vision

People do their best work when they understand *why* they are doing the work. Why does your organization exist? Your people, who contribute to the success of the organization, will be more effective when they are moving toward the same goals with the same intent.

Over 25 years ago, I had an information technology contract with Southwest Airlines (SWA). SWA's mission was—and still is—simply this:

> *The mission of Southwest Airlines is dedication to the highest quality of customer service delivered with a sense of warmth, friendliness, individual pride, and company spirit. We are committed to provide our employees a stable work environment with equal opportunity for learning and personal growth.*

When I logged into my computer, this was the first thing I saw on the screen. The mission was printed on small cards, about the size of a business card, and made available at all the administrative assistants' desks. The mission was framed and hung every 20 feet or so in the hallways of SWA's corporate headquarters. It was etched on glass two stories high behind the security desk in the corporate headquarters' lobby. There was never any doubt as to the mission of SWA on the part of employees or visitors. The behavior of SWA's employees reflected the mission in their dedication to the customer and the way they treated each other on the job.

The foundation of the GSD program is articulated in its mission, its creed, and its values. These three cornerstones appear every day in both written and oral form. There is never a question about why the class is being held, or why instructors commit their personal time to this organization.

Every day of the class, the morning operational briefing occurs at 6:30 a.m. The briefing begins with a review of the mission and objectives and why they are important:

> *To prevent death and injury by training firefighters to be adaptable and to develop critical decision making skills in high stress environments.*

The instructors know the mission; it hasn't changed. However, the instructor pool changes during the week, as many instructors can only come to the training for a couple of days at a time. Emphasizing the mission each day serves as a continual renewal of commitment for each Smoke Diver. This is part of a strategy to keep the instructors focused on the big picture, and aware of the influence and responsibility they have.

Candidates are required to know the creed when they arrive to take the class. They are asked to recite the Smoke Diver's Creed whenever asked, often in high-stress situations:

> *If I persist, if I continue to try, if I continue to charge forward, I will succeed. I will not hear those who weep and complain, for their disease is contagious. The prizes of life are at the end of each journey, not near the beginning, and it is not given to me to know how many steps are necessary in order to reach my goal. I will never consider defeat, and I will remove from my vocabulary such*

words as quit, cannot, unable, impossible, failure, and retreat, for these are the words of fools and cowards. When my thoughts beckon my tired body homeward, I will resist the temptation to depart. I will try again. I will make one more attempt to close with victory, and if that fails, I will make another. When others cease their struggle, then mine will begin, and my harvest will be full.

The mission and creed are supported by the core values, which are called "Nuts and Bolts:"

- Competence
- Honor
- Integrity
- Mental toughness
- Servant leadership
- Commitment

The core values represent the building of character and foster a sense of responsibility among Smoke Divers. These values are promoted during the week-long training through the telling of stories about firefighters who gave their lives in service to their communities. The class drills are based on line of duty deaths and near misses, in both the fire service and the military. The instructors tell the stories and then show the candidates various methods that could be used to recover from a similar situation. Candidates are given the leeway to think critically and to come up with a better way.

The final drill of the week is also called "Nuts and Bolts" to reinforce the learning of the week. Candidates are required to search a smoke-filled building for a bolt, and a series of washers and nuts. The bolt and each washer and nut corresponds to the core values of the program. If the candidate does the search correctly, the candidate will assemble the washers and nuts on the bolt in the correct order.

Communication in Emerging Incidents

Communication is not just about words. It is about tone and meaning. In the uniformed services, effective communication is critical in managing emerging incidents. The mandate is to remain calm, even when the world is on fire and people are in trouble. One firefighter I interviewed talked about how he listened to recordings of incidents in an effort to learn how to keep his voice calm. In his early years, he noticed that his voice got higher and faster as the incident progressed. As he matured as an officer, he would consciously strive to keep his voice calm and measured. This is an excellent example of active self-awareness.

Communication must be clear and accurately reflect the scene, including what is seen, felt, and heard. If it is a fire scene, each person is responsible for reporting back to the incident commander (IC) all aspects of their situational experience. The standard procedure is for the IC to do a 360 size-up; that is, they walk around the scene to get their initial impression of where the fire is, the color of the smoke (which can indicate the composition of what is burning), where the sources of water are, the construction of the structure, the terrain, how the weather might impact the scene, and so on. His or her communication about conditions of the scene must be clear, and unencumbered by emotion.

The IC relies on his or her team to provide updates to the knowledge of conditions he or she has already obtained, and which may have already changed in a very short period of time.

Therefore, each team member must be just as clear and concise in their reporting as the IC.

Firefighters have told me about incident commanders who scream when things get chaotic on the fireground. This does not instill confidence; it imparts the feeling of a loss of control to those listening to the communication. Remaining calm in the face of chaos is a skill, just like anything else. Learning what information to provide in the moment and how to convey that information is just as important as how to bail out of a window on an upper floor when you are cut off from any other means of escape.

To this end, the GSD program teaches candidates how to report a Mayday situation from the very beginning of the class. This exercise is incorporated into multiple drills, so that by the end of the class, the candidate can maintain a level of confidence in knowing exactly how to report when he or she is in trouble.

The program also gives students the opportunity to practice reporting incidents by showing videos of structures that are on fire or showing smoke. Each student is given the opportunity to report the scene as if he or she has just arrived and has to make all the decisions associated with the scenario, such as where to tie in to a water source, whether to search the structure, whether to attempt to knock down the fire, and/or how to prepare for the next-in apparatus. Other students in the class are encouraged to make suggestions and contribute to the decisions based on what they see. Given that on a real scene, everyone sees things just a bit differently, this collaborative style of communication helps paint a more complete and accurate picture of what is actually happening in the incident.

Communication at the scene of an incident is paramount, but needs to happen at all levels, in all situations, beginning with the individual. When we are at peace with ourselves, we are more confident and better able to operate in the context of the team, whether it is on the fireground, in the fire house, with our families, or in the world in general.

Communication with the Self

While there is no religious component within the GSD program, there are plenty of opportunities for both candidates and instructors to be self-reflective and even spiritual. How a person connects with Source (whatever he or she calls that Source) is a very personal thing. The GSD program is difficult, mentally and physically. Participants break away whenever possible to rest, contemplate, meditate, and pray. This is not an organized part of the program. It happens organically. Candidates and instructors honor the process by only interrupting an individual's contemplation when it is time to move to the next task or drill. It is quite beautiful to watch. Because this is an expected process, the spiritual energy among the participants contributes to and strengthens the connections among them. This tends to not be a topic of conversation. However, allowing each other to do what is necessary to spiritually recharge enables each individual to participate more fully.

Team Communication

Peter Drucker wrote in *Management Challenges for the 21st Century* that people must take responsibility for their relationships. To be effective, we need to "understand the people with whom we work and on whom we depend, and to make use of their strengths, their ways of working, and their values." We also need to "take responsibility for communications." It is every person's responsibility to tell co-workers how he or she prefers to receive information. Conversely, it is also every person's responsibility to ask co-workers how they want to receive information. When we each take responsibility for how people prefer to receive information and we honor that preference, misinterpretation of communication will be kept to a minimum.[89]

Both teams and individuals work more optimally when they have purpose. Leaders who communicate the vision and the mission establish meaning for individuals and teams in whatever environment they are working.[90] Individuals who actively practice self-awareness and who strive to continuously improve their own interpersonal skills contribute to the effectiveness of the team. These individuals, such as Steve Strawderman in the Kyle Wilson LODD and Mike McNamee in the Worcester Six incident, often become the stabilizing force in emergent incidents. Both these men are highly self-aware and committed to self-improvement in every aspect of their lives. Self-aware individuals serve as models for others to emulate, which ultimately results in team, organization, department, and professional success, while instilling a sense of honor and commitment to service.

Commit to a Stable Infrastructure

The very definition of an emergent situation refers to the sense of chaos and unpredictability on a moment-by-moment basis. Having a sound infrastructure enables the ability to focus on

---

[89] Drucker, 1999
[90] Pink, 2009

the changing environment without having to be concerned with tools, systems, and other operational aspects being in working order. Organizations cannot expect the best work of their people when the technology or the physical assets get in the way of efficiency.

In addition, people need to be trained to know what tools to use in a given situation. For example, firefighters need to be able to calculate water-flow throughput for the various nozzles and hoses at their disposal. In addition, they need to be able to recognize when the appropriate hose size should be used, based on fireground conditions. They need to know how to use the appropriate reporting systems, such as using the communication system to report fireground conditions, or using MS Word to write a report. Organizations that ignore the need for appropriate overall training cannot expect their workers to be able to do their best.

Infrastructure is the ultimate responsibility of administrative leaders who understand what the people serving the public need to do their jobs. These leaders must straddle the political line between those who are towing the financial line at the government council level and the departments they represent. This is not an easy—nor appreciated—task, and is often misunderstood by people on both sides of the political fence. However, there is no excuse for lack of knowledgeable advocacy on the part of administrative leadership. Not having the very best infrastructure can result in loss of life in both the community and the fire service. A public servant should never have to be concerned that he or she is working with equipment that is inferior, inadequate, or not in working order.

Infrastructure Components

There are four components of infrastructure as shown below in Figure 8:

Figure 8: 4 Components of Infrastructure

- Physical assets (buildings, apparatus, computers, tools, and equipment appropriate to the types of service to which the organization responds, personal protective equipment [PPE], etc.).
- Systems (both systemic processes and the supporting software that enables them).
- People to maintain and support both the assets and the systems.
- Knowledge management processes that support the activities of maintaining and operating the infrastructure and the overall work of the organization (e.g., living documentation in the form of standard operating procedures, after-action reports, and other decision-support information).

These components need to be in place for all aspects of the organization:

- Community response
- Communication systems
- Learning support
- Health and well-being monitoring and support
- Physical protection
- Knowledge management
- Attention to processes
- Administrative/management processes.

Physical Assets

Infrastructure includes the structures where we spend much of our lives as workers. I've been in many corporate environments that are nothing more than video-monitored cubicle farms. These environments are depressing, and not conducive to collaboration. There is very little natural light or privacy. Conference rooms are sparse, and have to be reserved in advance. When the reservation system doesn't work, workers waste time finding space to collaborate, which often causes conflicts between workers that sometimes become incendiary and contentious.

Organizations that create such cold, monitored environments convey to their workers that they are not trusted. This establishes an "us vs. them" environment in which no one enjoys working. We spend at least one third of our lives in the workplace. The workplace should be a place people want to be, where they enjoy both the environment and the work they do.

Because firefighters actually *live* in fire stations, these buildings should not only feel like home, they should facilitate activities that range from communal to alone time, as well as incorporate training and eating spaces.

During an incident, the command center is home. This is where command and support staff live, work, and make the hard decisions. The command center can be anywhere the command staff has the best overall view of the incident. It can be located in an office in a fixed building (such as a tower on the training ground), a mobile vehicle equipped with its own power and computers, a battalion chief's SUV, or a tent on top of a mountain. One of Georgia's sheriff departments lends its beautiful, well-appointed, internet-enabled command tractor-trailer to the GSD program during each class.

Equipment used to teach the GSD class is donated by other fire departments, the Georgia Fire Academy, the Dalton Fire Department, and even sponsors, like Georgia Fire & Rescue Supply. The instructors in the GSD program consider themselves to be stewards of all this donated equipment. They strive to return the equipment in better condition than when they received it. People and organizations who donate their equipment understand this, which is why they continue to donate the equipment from year to year.

Systems

In addition to physical assets, systems are critical. For example, on April 27, 2011, an EF4 tornado, with winds up to 174 miles per hour, touched down in Catoosa County, Alabama. This storm killed seven people, injured 30 more, and damaged or obliterated more than 75 homes. The incident management team had to create a communication plan. Catoosa County had a new communication system that ran at 800 MHz, but Mutual Aid was on another system (VHF). Together they decided to use a modal bridge to connect the two systems in real time. This shows large-scale, command-level situation awareness, collaboration, and creativity among the groups working this incident.

The counterpoint to this mandate is that you need to train for the situation with unstable infrastructure. Take, for example, training for taking off and landing a fighter jet on the deck of a Naval flight carrier, navigating 30-foot swells in the North Atlantic in the middle of the night. The experienced fighter pilot knows the mechanics of landing the plane. However, as he or she lines up the landing approach, the orientation of the deck changes. Not only can the ship appear to be rocking back and forth, it can be rolling from side to side. The pilot's brain tries to compensate for the instability, but even the instability constantly changes. The minute the pilot thinks he or she is about to land, the back of the deck could rise out of the water, causing the plane to crash into it and killing the pilot. The only way to prepare for this scenario is to do it over and over. This is the ultimate in learning what to do when patterns you *think* you recognize are constantly changing. Even the support people on the flight deck have to be prepared for any scenario.

If an incident is time sensitive, then commanders keep things simple and go by their training and experience. However, if the incident is bigger than a single-structure fire, for example, command uses the Incident Command System. In the case of the Georgia Smoke Diver program, the organization uses the Incident Command System to run the class for planning and execution. This offers a stable framework and infrastructure for emergent, innovative decision making.

When systems break down, what is your back up plan? Do your people understand the command structure, and who is in charge of what? Do they know what to do when their systems and equipment are not working? Is there a protocol that they are supposed to follow, and are they trained on this protocol?

The individual firefighter shouldn't have to know everything, but each person needs to understand what to do when something breaks down, whether it is to attempt to correct the problem on the spot or to report the issue to someone with specific expertise. While it is practically impossible to imagine every scenario that may need resolution, it is important to think of as many situations as possible, put in place standard operating procedures for handling these situations, and train both staff and personnel on these procedures. This effort should be done at a time that is not emergent. This is the essence of readiness.

Monitoring Progress

Monitoring progress and making necessary adjustments in real time is essential to an organization's relevance and ability to respond to those who benefit from the organization's existence. This requires multi-level vigilance on the part of the organization's leadership. In other words, situation awareness is as important to leadership as it is to the individual. Just as awareness is experienced within the individual, situation awareness is concurrently internal and external.

In the GSD program, internal awareness refers to what happens during the class itself. Leadership must exercise vigilance to the inner workings of the class: the instructors, the students, the teams to which they are all assigned, and the dynamics on the training ground.

External awareness refers to the events and teachings available outside the class, such as training advances, Underwriters Laboratories studies, and incidents that occur in the fire service which they can use to modify and improve GSD training.

Internal Organizational Situation Awareness

In the GSD program, there are five standing meetings every day.

- At 6:30, the leadership conducts the morning briefing with the instructors to go over the day's drills in the context of potential weather conditions, safety considerations, and assignments.

- At 10:30, the leadership meets to discuss tactics, review the next day's activities, discuss any problems that happened that morning while setting up, discuss assignments for the next day, and change processes as appropriate.

- At 14:00, the leadership team meets again to recalibrate and discuss issues that need to be addressed.

- After the class is finished for the day, the leadership team meets with the instructors again to communicate any information pertinent to the day's decisions and the next day's schedule.

- After the final instructor briefing, the leadership team meets to prepare for the next day's morning briefing and discuss any last-minute changes.

Meetings are not long. They are designed to address issues quickly, determine a resolution, make assignments, and decide how the resolution will be communicated.

Attention to Process

Processes are the engine of an organization's work. However, they are continuously evolving. People find new and better ways to do the work of the organization. I've spent my life documenting processes and procedures in a variety of organizations. While documentation projects are often attempts to capture how the organization does its work, the resulting work product is often no more than a snapshot in time.

Processes continually evolve because, unless there is forced standardization, people will change the process to fit the circumstance. *Why* they make that change is what gets lost. If this tacit knowledge is not captured and codified, the organization is doomed to repeat the same errant processes over and over.

What is amazing about the GSD program is its ability to keep processes simple, and let them evolve naturally with the available technology. For example, when I began observing training in 2011, the instructors kept yellow cards and white cards in their pockets along with a pencil. The yellow cards were used to report the candidates' infractions. The white cards were used to suggest ideas for improvement. The instructors gave their cards to the Plans team (the administrative team within GSD), who sorted them and scanned them into the system. The coordinators in Plans would then print a report for the leadership at the end of the day.

At the fall 2016 class, this process had changed. By this time, the instructors all had smartphones. Chris Cook (GSD #383), who manages the Plans team, created an online form for the instructors to access on their smartphones. When they input a candidate infraction or a new idea, the system is automatically updated. This completely eliminated the need to scan all the paper into the system.

Knowledge Management

Knowledge management consists of all the written and visual documentation, including information about what happened during the class, standard operating procedures, templates for agendas and communication, photographs and videos, ideas that instructors submit during the class, and data about each of the candidates. Chris Cook is in charge of keeping all these information artifacts maintained and categorized.

Standard operating procedures (SOPs) are foundational to any organization. They spell out how the organization executes its mission. What many organizations do not realize, though, is that SOPs are not static. They should be living documents that reflect the decisions of the leadership. It is important to strike a balance in the level of granularity within the SOPs. If the organization dictates every step of a process, maintenance of that SOP will be much more difficult than if the organization offers guidelines on how something should be done. However, you don't want to be so vague that processes and procedures are not executed consistently. Hiring a professional technical communicator to help with this balance will result in measurable dividends in the long run.

All of the standard operating procedures of the GSD program are documented and maintained on a regular basis. This is what has enabled them to assist Indiana to duplicate the program. However, it will be Indiana's responsibility to modify their SOPs over time as they change their program to suit their needs.

Another form of knowledge management is storytelling, although this is less formal. Some of the stories have been codified because they are used as the basis for some of the training, such as the Denver Drill. Codifying these stories helps to anchor the facts, which, in informal storytelling, tend to morph, expand, and contract. New elements enter the story, and over time, become "facts." Storytelling is an effective way to bind an organization to its "ancestral" knowledge. I will discuss this phenomenon in the next section.

Bind the Group

Have you ever worked with a group of people who seemed so connected that they finish each other's sentences? They move as one, like a well-oiled machine. Each person takes responsibility for his or her own work and well-being, while also taking responsibility for communication with others on the team. This is what team flow looks like. What facilitates this is a common history and culture, trust, and respect among team members. The organization feels almost tribal.

For some strange reason, the idea of tribalism has evolved to have negative meaning. When tribalism becomes territorial and defensive, and begins to consciously separate itself by dehumanizing those not in the tribe, I would agree that the idea of tribalism is quite negative.

However, I have witnessed a different form of tribalism in the GSD program. While the members of this tribe are tight with one another within the program, one of the things that binds them is the common focus of *service to others*, both inside and outside the tribe. This idea permeates all aspects of the program, from the mission, to the creed, to the speeches given during the week, to the informal storytelling that occurs while individuals are warming their hands by the burn barrels. Everyone is united around the idea that they are there to make firefighters better so they can better serve their communities, and so they can go home at the end of the day. Period.

They are territorial only in defending their brand. I learned this the hard way, at the last GSD training. After attending 11 trainings and knowing that only the people who have been through the program were allowed to purchase the GSD t-shirts, you would think that I would also know this would include the "GA. SMOKE DIVER" rocker patch, which is part of the brand.

Just before the training, my ancient black hoodie gave up the ghost. I needed a new zip-up hoodie. In the past, this item of clothing wasn't available at the GSD store. There was a new person selling all of the memorabilia. This new seller said that she could get a zip-up hoodie for me for $20. Done!

She asked me what I wanted on it. I jokingly said, "The rocker. But I'm not sure I'm allowed to have that." She said, "Sure, I can do that. Do you want your name on the other side of the zipper on the front?" "Yes!" I was very excited that this was okay. She had it for me by the end of the week of training. I was so proud to wear something that connected me to the group, I wore it to the informal graduation. I showed it to Smoke Daddy. He said, "Who got you that?" I proudly said, "I did." I guess I was so excited and happy about my prized possession that he didn't have the heart to tell me that I couldn't wear the rocker. He waited about three weeks. Then, he called me at home. He gently told me, "We are going to have to take the hoodie back, but we will replace it with something special." I was crestfallen, but I told him I wouldn't wear the hoodie and

that I would give it back to him. He left me with the feeling of
excited expectation of what they are going to come up with for
me. They never disappoint.

The brand is one thing, but when it comes to the program itself,
the leaders of the GSD program are more than willing to share
their SOPs, methods, lessons learned, staff, and resources to
help that new program get up and running. They have proven
this in the cases of Indiana and Oklahoma, when they wanted
to investigate duplicating the program in their own states. GSD
is all about sharing the knowledge and collaborating with other
groups to support the mission of helping firefighters be better at
what they do.

Binding the group through a sense of purpose, accompanied by
the sense of mutual trust and support, fosters accountability.
The glue for a bound organization is trust. Cultivate trust with
ritual, storytelling, laughter, and collaboration.

Ritual

David Rhodes is a master of ritual. He understands that
emotions help bind the group, and that making meaning out of
seemingly everyday moments builds trust and respect. He
knows intuitively that ritual binds the group. There are dozens
of regular rituals, both formal and informal, that occur during
GSD week.

One of the most powerful rituals occurs on Wednesday morning,
around 10 a.m. Candidates gather around Smoke Daddy.
Rhodes stands in front of a door that was constructed of pieces
from three houses, each of which was the location of a Georgia
line of duty death. Each part of the door displays its original
house number. Rhodes tells the stories of the lost firefighters

who entered the homes from the front door, but who didn't come out the same way. In an impassioned voice, he then hones in on his main message:

> "Our customers don't have a choice when they call 911. They get whoever is on duty. How *dare* we be anything but the best we can be... You give that father another day with his son. You make it possible for that grandmother to watch her granddaughter graduate from high school..."

These are the words Rhodes uses to impress on candidates the importance of what the GSD program is all about: service. This is an emotional speech, often drawing tears from those who hear it. It hits home. It is the essence of why men and women become firefighters. Chief Rhodes has a knack for saying just the right thing in the right moment. This is because he lives and breathes his own commitment to live a life of service.

Wednesday in the Georgia Smoke Diver training program is a pivotal day for students. The big drill of that day is called Five Evolutions. The essence of the drill is that students enter the burn building from the second floor of a three-story building. Inside the building are five lines of fire hoses that instructors have strategically wound throughout the building like a knotted chain in a jewelry box. The student has to find his or her way out of the building by following one of those hoses. They have to come out of the building following the same hose on which they started. They then have to go back into the building on the next hose line, and repeat until they have followed all five lines out of the building. They have to do this on two 30-minute air packs. After each evolution, they have to wait in line for their turn to go on the next line.

Just prior to the drill, Smoke Daddy weaves in and out of the line quietly speaking to each student individually. Heads nod and Smoke Daddy moves to the next student. From my vantage point as an observer, this ritual appears to calm the student. I have taken many pictures of the students standing in line. Their faces are telling in terms of emotion and state of mind. When I ask what they were thinking as they stood in line, responses are very similar: "I was praying." "I was getting my head right." "I was clearing my mind."

Knowledge Sharing and Storytelling

In addition to eliciting an emotional response, stories create a common history. Hero and survivor stories facilitate leadership, help with positive change, and help maintain morale. Storytelling provides the explanation for events, which helps reduce stress and uncertainty. The act of storytelling binds the organization in a multitude of ways. It reinforces organizational values. Sharing stories about incidents with others helps deepen the knowledge pool by enabling others to understand techniques, strategies, and tactics for dealing with similar situations.[91]

The act of revisiting what happened in an incident is what Weick calls "retrospective sensemaking."[92] Storytelling construction consists of a beginning, middle, and end.[93] Sensemaking construction parallels storytelling through disruption, transformation, and solution.[94]

---

[91] Kopp, Nikolovska, Desiderio, & Guterman, 2011

[92] Weick, 1988

[93] Kopp, Nikolovska, Desiderio, & Guterman, 2011

[94] Weick, 1995

The best examples of sensemaking in the fire service are after action reports, which serve as the official record of incidents. Anyone can go to the National Firefighter Near Miss Reporting System[95] to learn about specific incidents or to submit after action reports for others to review. Submissions are scrubbed of the names of individuals who made critical decisions to minimize the tendency we all have to second-guess the decisions made and to minimize blame. These reports lay out the framework of the incident (disruption), describe the decisions made and what happened as a result of the decisions (transformation), and suggest modifications in training, procedures, and culture to prepare for future incidents that may be similar (solution).

There will always be those who second-guess the decisions of those intimately involved in an incident. However, most firefighters understand the idea that, unless you were there and had all the information the decision maker had, you really don't have the right to second-guess the decision maker.

When firefighters return to the station, they discuss what happened. Every person on scene has a different point of view geographically and a different perspective about what they believe happened. Consolidating everyone's perceptions, helps create a three-dimensional story or slide that each individual can use in future experiences. This activity can also help point out what training needs to be done. Every squad on every shift in every fire house has its own set of oral histories. This rehashing of events helps combat hindsight bias, which can

---

[95] www.firefighternearmiss.com

cause you to evaluate what happened during an incident based on the outcome, rather than the quality of the decisions.[96]

I recently visited a station in Forsyth County, Georgia. Based on the incidents to which they had been responding, the firefighters determined they needed to train more on how to bail out of an upper story in a house. In addition, they recognized that many of the houses they served had basements, where they could become entrapped if they fell through the floor. They needed to train on how to extricate themselves and others from the basement. They built a prop in the engine bay to accommodate both these scenarios. The window in the prop had a removable frame that simulated the basement window scenario, when the frame was removed. Replacing the frame in the prop had the effect of raising the level of the window to simulate an escape through an upper-story window.

Role of Laughter

One of the most enjoyable elements of being around Georgia Smoke Divers is the amount of laughter that permeates everything they do. While they can turn serious in a heartbeat, much of the day, in between instructing and monitoring candidates, is spent telling stories, pranking one another, and creating new funny memories, which often appear in the next day's morning briefing. Stories morph and get embellished over time; they get repeated over and over in subsequent classes. The stories act as inside jokes. In addition, it is impossible to just observe this group without eventually becoming part of the lore. Everything is free game. For example, this is a story where I was the butt of the joke:

---

[96] Kahneman, 2011

It was Thursday, Heat Day. The weather was miserable outside. Most of the activity on the training ground was inside the burn building. I had work to do for a client. I decided that I would rather be inside and billable. I went into the firehouse kitchen to work. Around 2:00, I realized I was very drowsy and decided to stop for a bit and take a nap. No one had been in the fire station for hours. I decided I would just take advantage of the quiet time.

The next day, during the morning briefing, Smoke Daddy displayed a picture of me napping. He had found me sleeping and quietly snapped a picture of me. The guys just howled with laughter. Here was their researcher, asleep on the job, while they were outside freezing in the rain and snow.

As a result of this tendency to single out people in stories, Smoke Divers are careful to not give away sensitive, personal information that could ultimately end up as the subject of a story or the foundation for a prank. In another example, somehow someone found out that one of his fellow Smoke Divers, whom I will call G, was afraid of clowns. The word got around. Another Smoke Diver, whom I will call W, had a clown mask—one that covered the entire head. No one knew the extent of G's fear of clowns, initially.

G was building smoke for one of the drills. This is a tough job, which requires that the firefighter be in full gear. He was diligently moving in and out of the burn building carrying armfuls of hay to burn. W put on the clown mask and entered the building on the opposite side, so that when G went into the building full of smoke, he would see a clown mysteriously appearing through the smoke. G almost hurt himself, flipping head over heels trying to get out of the building. He later told me he didn't remember moving. He only remembered that all of a sudden, he found himself on the other side of the training ground. This confirmed G's utter and complete fear to the other instructors, which subsequently egged them on to invent new ways to frighten G. The stories and ensuing laughter, which I have to say on the surface really bothered me, served to bond the group even closer together. The really interesting thing is that G keeps returning as an instructor for the class, knowing that there is a strong possibility that someone will pull another clown trick on him. This speaks to G's character and commitment to the program.

There is an odd feeling that when you are singled out within a story, it is an expression of love and respect. Laughter is the auditory equivalent of a hug of the grandest proportions.

Storymaking and storytelling result in opportunities for laughter. Because the mission is so intense—literally focusing on life and death—laughter is the logical and natural way to balance the seriousness of the day.

Power of Collaboration

Collaboration happens at the team level, as well as the organizational level. During the GSD training, the collaboration is easy to see as teams live, eat, and go through drills together. They encourage each other and work together to solve problems. This bond ultimately creates life-long friendships.

GSD is in the process of supporting efforts to make both the Indiana Smoke Diver and Oklahoma Smoke Diver programs viable. However, they each will evolve over time, based on the needs of the fire service in their respective states. The GSD program encourages them to do just that. GSD is not a franchise. There is no effort or process used to control other states' programs other than to promote the core principles of the program. GSD is fine with the organic nature of this approach. Leaders from all three programs will continue to assist each other by providing instructors for training and through knowledge sharing. The cross-pollination of ideas and leadership will enable the sustainability and longevity of all three programs.

In addition, here in Georgia, there is a great deal of GSD leadership overlap in the various external training programs, such as Georgia F.L.A.M.E.S. and AXIOMS of Leadership. Collaboration is what has enabled GSD to spread its "Good Word" throughout the fire service, binding them to other organizations, such as, the Fire Department Instructors' Conference; the Underwriters Laboratories studies; the Georgia Fire Academy; departments around the United States, who have sent their firefighters through the program; and many other external organizations.

This outward focus binds GSD to those with whom they work. This collaborative model is an extension of the Leadership by Example mandate. They consistently demonstrate to the world their commitment to their purpose.

What's Your Number?

Numbers are significant in the GSD program. In Smoke Daddy's Wednesday morning speech, he talks about numbers: birthdays, the numbers on houses, the dates of our deaths. Numbers bind the group together. Each Smoke Diver is assigned a number as he or she graduates. This is nothing more than a sequential number indicating the order in which a class graduates. The sequence begins with the next sequential number following the last graduating class. The March 2015 class was the 50th Georgia Smoke Diver class, which graduated GSD numbers 909 through 920.

Many graduates came back for a reunion during this class, including GSD #1 (Dr. Cortez Lawrence, Department of Homeland Security, FEMA Emergency Management Institute, US Fire Administration) and GSD # 2 (Brenda "Nish" Willis, Chief of the Henry County, Georgia, Fire Department). Chiefs Lawrence and Willis designed the original GSD program based on the 1970s Florida Smoke Diver model.

On April 4, 2015, the GSD program lost one of its Lead Instructors, retired Deputy Chief of the Dalton Georgia Fire Department, Gary Baggett (GSD #283), in a motorcycle accident. At Gary's funeral, Smoke Daddy referenced Scott Millsap (also from Dalton and best friends with Gary) who was GSD #25. He pointed out that when you break down Gary's number as 2, 8, and 3, and subtract the 3 from the 8, you are left with a 2 and a 5 (25). Adding this number to Millsap's number 25 gives you 50, which was the class GSD just graduated. The program is full of these types of numerical coincidences. Assigning meaning helps bind the group even more tightly together.

Honor Individual Creativity to Promote Innovation

While elements of the class stay the same, each class is an evolution of all the classes that came before it. While change occurs from class to class, it also occurs during the class from day to day.

The leadership encourages idea generation. All contributions and suggestions are considered with regard to usefulness and benefit to the students. Anyone can suggest changes to the program at any time. These ideas are reviewed by the command staff daily. Many of the approved changes are implemented immediately, with little fanfare. Other changes that require further research are implemented during the next class. Every suggestion is vetted. Submitters are informed as to the status of their suggestions. If a suggestion is rejected, the submitter is told why.

Changes also occur when events and new research in the fire service call for modification. For example, in September 2012, a student died in the Texas Smoke Diver program due to heat exhaustion. The Texas program is not related to the GSD program. However, there were a number of Georgia Smoke Divers assisting that class, and one who was actually a student. This incident had a ripple effect throughout training in the fire service. In fact, the GSD-sponsored Indiana Smoke Diver program was about to launch its first class in October 2012. Indiana fire chiefs were pulling students out of the ISD class, thinking it was related. There was a great deal of public relations work that had to occur to keep the ISD class on the calendar. The ISD leadership invited the chiefs to come observe the class; many of them did. The class was a success.

Because there were Georgia Smoke Divers at the Texas class, they were able to do a first-hand assessment of what happened and make recommendations to the GSD program. As a result, GSD changed its procedures on how they paid attention to a student's physical well-being. While the instructors were always cognizant of a student's physical state, they used to give more emphasis to what the student told them when asked, "How are you feeling?" If the student thought he or she was okay to continue, the instructor would most likely allow it. The new procedures are reiterated every morning during the morning briefing. In addition, they added small pools full of ice in strategic places on the training ground to facilitate a quick cool down of a student in case of overheating.

GSD regularly monitors and studies LODD reports, injury reports from real incidents and training incidents, and constantly makes adjustments to minimize risk. Georgia Fire-Rescue owner, Deacon, and Lead Instructor, Jeff Whidby (GSD # 501), stays current on new firefighting technology and brings the latest thermal imaging cameras, hose lines, nozzles, and other equipment to the class. He then skillfully teaches candidates how to use this new technology.

The leadership is constantly looking for new ways to honor creativity. For example, the deacon designation is relatively recent. The Board of Elders felt there were a number of lead instructors who have demonstrated commitment over a long period of time. The elders wanted to formally recognize this commitment. In 2012, they voted to change the organizational structure to include the role of deacon. There was no conflict or debate around this decision. It felt like the natural progression of the organization.

Use Positive Motivation Techniques

Does your organization have a strategy for motivating its employees? People feel motivated when their personal reason for being aligns with the organization's purpose. In addition, people are not necessarily motivated by money or things. Money and things are short-lived. The joy associated with this type of reward dissipates quickly, and is often replaced with a sense of entitlement. People come to expect the bonus or the trophy and are upset when, even after doing mediocre work, they don't get it.

According to Daniel Pink, "When contingent rewards aren't involved, or when incentives are used with the proper deftness, performance improves and understanding deepens."[97] Assuming that people are being compensated with a living wage, initially, people performing in service to an articulated higher purpose achieve more than those who perform for tangible rewards. Therefore, it is important they understand why they do what they do.

Mo Squad

During the first GSD training I attended, I noticed that during the morning briefing, when the assignments were made, there were a number of instructors assigned to the Mo Squad and nothing else. I asked Smoke Daddy, "What is the Mo Squad?" He told me these are the instructors whose only job is to motivate candidates. Senior lead instructors make up the Mo Squad.

Imagine having a team of people in your organization whose *sole* responsibility is to motivate people.

Many organizations have mentoring programs that serve this purpose, but the success of these programs depends on individual commitment by the mentors and consistency in how people are mentored. Again, this gets back to rewards. What is the motivation of the mentors? Do they mentor for the purposes of wanting recognition for themselves, or do they mentor because of the intrinsic value to the growth and

[97] Pink, 2009

sustainability of the organization, as well as their individual commitment to growth for themselves and others? Do they mentor for the sheer joy of helping another human being? Or do they do it for the potential bonus, or to put it on their resume?

People know when someone is genuine in his or her intentions just by watching his or her behaviors. Being disingenuous and selfish is a hard thing to mask. Mentoring is different from encouraging, or being a cheerleader for someone else. Mentoring is a skill that by its very nature, has to be selfless. Training for how to mentor is key to running a successful, consistent mentoring program in an organization.

Mentoring starts within the self. We must be secure within ourselves to mentor someone else. This doesn't necessarily mean that we know everything; in fact, it means that when we don't know the answer, we are secure enough in our own skin to be able to say, "I don't know. Let's find out together."

Just as it is the firefighter's job to save his or her own life first in a life-threatening situation, mentors must be able to be their own motivators before they can help motivate others. This goes back to setting the example for those who follow you.

Motivation Strategies

Consciously setting and communicating motivation strategies and tactics within the organization helps with consistent application of those strategies across the board. There may be times where some tactics are more appropriate than others.

There is a distinct strategy followed by the Mo Squad in the GSD training. In the daily briefing of the instructors, Smoke

Daddy reminds the instructors as a whole what the motivation strategy is for that day.

Because this is a program designed to help firefighters make better decisions in stressful situations, the Mo Squad pushes hard early in the week. On the surface, tactics feel almost mean, and borderline personal. These tactics begin during PT and last until the end of the day, when various punishments (such as running laps in full turn-out gear) for infractions that happened during the day are meted out. A tactic can be anything from words that tease, to a look from one of the senior instructors, to a serious reprimand resulting in some form of punishment.

There is so much joy and laughter on the training ground that when a serious reprimand occurs, it often takes me by surprise. Even the air around the instructors and candidates seems to thicken.

The first time I observed this phenomenon, I was joking around with some of the instructors who were waiting their turn to help with an evolution in the burn building. All of a sudden, a group of candidates were marched away from the burn building and told to take a knee on the ground next to where I was sitting. The instructors I was talking to just moments before were immediately on their feet, surrounding the candidates. It happened so fast, I was taken aback. The team of candidates evidently had been repeatedly executing the drill wrong, even after they had been corrected over and over.

The instructors they were working with were doing all the talking. The instructors with whom I had been interacting were acting as a very intimidating wall of support. Their ability to switch from lightheartedness to seriousness was stunning. Remember that feeling when you were a kid, when your father or mother reprimanded you for doing something wrong? Multiply that feeling by ten. That was how I, as an observer, felt. My heart went out to the candidates, but I also felt the intense frustration of the instructors. But let's put this in perspective: This is their life on the line. This training is serious; it is about life and death.

Visual and Physical Motivation

PT is a telling time of day. Candidates are instructed to line up in a specific place on the training ground. They are told that if an emergency happens while they are in training, they are to return to this place so that they can be accounted for. This place on the training ground becomes their home for the week.

In the story I just recounted, imagine the candidates sitting on the ground surrounded by instructors, who are standing. Remember the ratio of instructors to students is three to one. In addition, many of the instructors are very intimidating by the sheer nature of their physical appearance. They also take great joy in making themselves look even more intimidating. For example, they will wear clothes that enhance their size or perceived meanness, such as wearing t-shirts with the sleeves torn off in very cold weather to reveal muscled arms covered in tattoos. One instructor wears a leather top hat that makes him look even taller than his six-foot-four frame.

To top it all off, the instructors don't just dictate and lead the PT exercises; they do the exercises with the class. There will often be pools of water on the training ground where they are doing PT. The instructors, as well as the candidates, can't avoid getting wet and cold. Even though the instructors are yelling at the candidates and making them do the hardest of exercises (think burpees, a.k.a., up and downs) in full gear, the instructors do not ask students to do anything they aren't willing to do themselves. This is a striking instance of leading by example.

Early in the week, it is easy to tell how well the class is going to do by the way they stack their gear while in formation. The instructors want to see gear stacked neatly and shoes lined up. You should be able to stand at the end of one of the lines of gear and shoes and see that they are a straight line. This seemingly simple task becomes a great (and easy) source of material that can be used to tease and cajole the candidates. However, this is also a great way to impress upon the candidates the importance of paying attention to detail in each moment. Sloppy care of equipment, lack of attention to order, and not lining up with others on the team can result in loss of life on the fireground. Failure to comply with this mandate can result in ridicule that the candidate won't forget.

At the end of one difficult class day, the instructors were so aggravated that the candidates just couldn't get the concept of order, they stacked all the gear and shoes on a huge pile while the candidates were running laps. When the candidates returned to formation, they found all their gear jumbled up in an enormous mess. They were exhausted. But they had to find all their gear before they could go eat dinner and go to bed. The next morning, they had no problem lining up their gear in perfect formation.

Shift to Positive Motivation

Eventually, the tone of the encouragement turns from "What makes you think you are good enough to be here?" to "Come on. You got this!'" The shift is so subtle it is almost imperceptible. You have to be paying attention to see and hear the difference. By the middle of the week, those candidates who remain are truly committed, determined to make it through to the end of the class. They have bonded with one another. Motivation comes from within the cohort, in spite of the instructors. Often, when their classmates have to run laps for some infraction that happened during the day, the entire class will run the laps in support of the classmate getting punished.

When the instructors make their subtle shift to a more positive form of inspiration, the bonds extend outward from the cohort to include the instructors. The level of mutual respect for one another is outwardly visible. The shift is elegant and beautiful in its manifestation. The feeling of commitment and respect permeates the entire class.

Motivation for Those Who Don't Make It

People drop the class for a variety of reasons. Some have to discontinue the class for medical reasons. For example, they become dehydrated. Some get injured. Some just go home without warning, because the class was not what they expected. When a candidate cannot continue for any reason, the instructors conduct an exit interview. The candidate completes a form stating the reasons for discontinuing the course. The leadership uses this feedback when considering changes in the program.

Then one of the senior instructors goes over what the candidate has written with the candidate. The instructor is careful to use positive language in the interview. There is no mention of the candidate being a failure. There is talk about what is learned from failure. The instructor explains that this is a tough program and encourages the candidate to try again. If the candidate failed to complete a particular drill successfully, the instructor gives him or her ideas as to how to prepare for the drill in the future. The candidate is sent home with positive words of encouragement.

There is, however, a negative side of this. When a candidate isn't stepping up or taking responsibility for his actions, no amount of positive motivation will help. In one such extreme case, the candidate in question would not pull his weight at all. He wasn't committed to the program, but he wanted the Smoke Diver designation. He constantly caused his team to show up late to the training ground. He complained incessantly. He barely completed the minimum standards required of each drill. He single-handedly slowed down training evolutions and caused delays for the entire program. Finally, his teammates complained to the leadership about this man's attitude. Leadership counseled him. He insisted he was committed to finishing the program. His attitude began to impact everyone in a negative way. Finally, near the end of the week, when he continued to ignore one of the instructors on the proper way to do a hose hoist, the instructor failed him and sent him packing. During his exit interview, which I observed, he wouldn't take responsibility for any of his failures. In fact, he wanted to blame others for his inability to execute the drills. The interviewer remained professional and even offered constructive ideas for preparing for the class in the future, if he decided he wanted to come back and take the class again. The candidate left angry, but after he left, you could feel the weight of his negative presence lift from the training ground.

Facilitate Team Flow

As a manager, it is important to be able to initiate your own flow state and equally as important to recognize and facilitate the abilities of the people on your team to initiate their flow states. To do this requires your attention and the ability to observe objectively. Learn about your people at an individual level. What are their individual goals? What are their hopes and dreams? What are they afraid of? Ask yourself how each person fits into the scheme of things you have to achieve in your role as leader. Does that person need help? Would he or she be better served in another role? What are his or her strengths and weaknesses on the team? What does he or she love to do? Find a place on the team or in the organization where he or she can do what he or she loves. If that person is doing what he or she loves to do, he or she will be less likely to leave the organization, and will take joy in doing his or her best for the team.

Deliberately introduce variation to workflow. Csikszentmihalyi uses the example of how moving through a museum room to room fosters boredom. However, having people move through a connecting hall or bridge with different views (e.g., the ocean, the mountains, the city) will help the individual see the art in the next room with fresh eyes.[98]

Workflow is full of processes. Doing the same thing over and over again, day after day, increases boredom, even when, initially, we may have enjoyed the activity. Breaking up the activity allows us to return to what needs to be done with a renewed mindset.

---

[98] Csikszentmihalyi, 2003

Csikszentmihalyi has recently teamed up Zsadany "Zad" Vecsey who is the Founder and CEO of an organization with offices in Hungary and in California called ALEAS Simulations, Inc. Together, they have produced a computer-based game called FLOW Leadership is Good Business™, or FLIGBY.

The game teaches people how to run a flow-based organization through a computer simulation. Their website describes the game as:

> a micro-simulation, which means that the dilemmas of various organizations are integrated into our framework story of the Californian Business called Turul Winery. Each event simulated in the course of the game is based on authentic situations from our business consulting experiences in organizational development.[99]

FLIGBY is based on Csikszentmihalyi's dimensions of flow-based leadership and provides quality, authentic data and feedback for your team. FLIGBY provides personalized feedback to anyone playing the game. The feedback is based on 90 decisions, with three or four options available for each decision. When you choose the least bad decision, your personality profile gets modified and tracked along Csikszentmihalyi's flow-based leadership dimensions.

The data will also be used to predict how people should be helped to work in flow, and to enable organizations to identify skills gaps among their team members. Currently, the simulation is only being used in business schools, and access to

---

[99] http://www.fligby.com

the data is limited to academics. The program is not meant to be a money-making proposition.[100]

Conclusion

Changing a culture and building a flow-based organization requires vigilance, deliberation, and attention to detail. Learn to recognize when you have normalized unsafe practices for the sake of tradition.[101] Often tradition is perpetuated by ostracizing anyone who is different or doesn't conform.

Firefighters know who they are at their core and understand their life purpose and mission. When you purposely live your life with this knowledge, you live authentically. You also take care of yourself—not in a narcissistic way, but in a way that recognizes that you cannot help others if you are not healthy in all aspects of your life.

When we separate ourselves through stereotyping and simple abstractions about others, "we're in danger of losing touch with the reality of our actual connections."[102] We cannot effectively live with each other and affect the social changes that need to happen when we live in isolation. When we are out of touch with our actual connections, we experience conflict. Those who are able to regulate themselves and be aware of their goals, even in the midst of conflict, can move their lives forward in a constructive way. However, if people lose sight of their goals in the midst of conflict, the motivation to self-regulate lessens. This can cause conflict to escalate. Being able to adapt goals and actions in creative ways can act as a cooling strategy for

---

[100] Seligman, 2003

[101] International Association of Fire Chiefs and U.S. Fire Administration, 2015

[102] Briggs & Peat, 1999

dealing with conflict.[103] Conflict management happens when conflicting parties recognize their interdependence.[104]

The underlying component is that of the individual's willingness to detach, and to be a servant leader: that is, someone who facilitates the growth of others through collaborative learning.[105] Servant leaders give without expectation of return.[106] However, by doing this, reciprocity occurs in unexpected ways, which ultimately helps to create community. Firefighters set the example for the rest of us by exercising detached compassion.

As a practical matter, one must be aware to practice detachment.[107] For example, firefighters must keep personal emotions under control. It is important for the firefighter to remain calm and act responsibly as a member of the emergency team. This is often not easy in the face of tragedy. Duty to act refers to the firefighter's responsibility to provide care, even when not on duty, without judgment. Firefighters "have a moral and ethical duty to act because of [their] special training and expertise."[108] This moral commitment to helping others helps the firefighter "believe that life is good and worth investing in."[109] This mindset enables firefighters to stay calm in the midst of critical situations and requires commitment and

[103] Mischel & DeSmet, 2000

[104] Watts, 1966

[105] Goerner et al., 2008

[106] Greenleaf, 1977

[107] *Ibid*

[108] American Academy of Orthopaedic Surgeons, 2002

[109] Taylor & Wolin, 2002

detachment from outcome, self, and emotion, as well as the ability to learn from the actions of self and others.[110]

The profession of firefighting is, by nature, a collaboration. It often takes courage to express one's own thoughts. "Courage is not the absence of despair; it is, rather, the capacity to move ahead in spite of despair."[111] No one does this better than those in the fire service. Living in this space requires the individual to be centered within. Authentic commitment arises from the centeredness. Commitment to authenticity takes courage.[112]

Firefighters exhibit all forms of courage: (a) physical courage, (b) moral courage, (c) social courage, and (d) creative courage. They are aware that effectiveness on the job and meeting the goal of safety for both the public and the individual firefighter depends on their own physical fitness and the fitness of their equipment.[113] This cultivates the ability to think with the body. Firefighters exhibit moral courage through their compassion and sensitivity with the suffering of others. They exhibit social courage when they risk their own psyches for the rest of us. The intimacy required to comfort a sobbing toddler pulled from beneath the body of the child's dead mother in the aftermath of a fatal car accident is unfathomable to the majority of us.[114] To be socially courageous requires the knowledge that we not know how the relationship with others will affect us.

Creative courage is the most difficult of the forms of courage, because it requires us to discover new meaning in the context of

---

[110] Senge, 1977

[111] May, 1975

[112] *Ibid*

[113] Smeby, 2006

[114] Strawderman, interview, 2009

an ever-evolving society.[115] The fire service profession is constantly changing as new knowledge is discovered. Firefighters construct knowledge through their experiences. As their knowledge changes, the way they interact with each other, their environment, and society changes. This occurs not only in what they know, but in the transforming structures of their knowledge.[116] The constant process of training, learning, and reviewing of past incidents is how the firefighter exhibits creative courage. "The need for creative courage is in direct proportion to the degree of change the profession is undergoing."[117] The fire service profession is in a state of perpetual change.

The big buzzword in leadership circles is *bravery*. Bravery isn't just willingness to go where others don't want to venture, or putting yourself in harm's way. Bravery is also about being emotionally vulnerable, being able to love without conditions, being able to forgive fully, living life with a purpose, and knowing that the world, and the universe, ultimately works in ways that pull toward the good.

Georgia Smoke Divers are the bravest people I know. They are happy, giving, loving people who have dedicated their lives to excellence in training firefighters. These firefighters love their jobs, families, communities, and each other with a fierceness that is unparalleled.[118]

We all can learn from their example. We all live on this tiny marble at the edge of an obscure galaxy at the edge of the universe. Our collective well-being is at stake. When any one of

---

[115] May, 1975

[116] W. I. Thompson, 1996

[117] May, 1975

[118] Glick-Smith, 2015

us suffers, we all suffer. It is in our own best interest to facilitate flow for all of those around us.

References

ALEAS Simulations, Inc. (2016, May 15). *About*. Retrieved from fligby: www.fligby.com

ALEAS Simulations, Inc.,. (2016, January 1). Retrieved from FLIGBY: http://www.fligby.com

Allison, M. T., & Duncan, M. C. (1988). Women, work, and flow. In M. Csikszentmihalyi, & I. S. Csikszentimihalyi (Eds.), *Optimal experience: Psychological studies of flow in consciousness* (pp. 118-137). Cambridge, UK: Cambridge University Press.

American Academy of Orthopaedic Surgeons. (2002). *Emergency: Care and transportation of the sick and injured* (8th ed.). (B. D. Browner, A. N. Pollak, & C. L. Gupton, Eds.) Sudbury, MA: Jones & Bartlett.

Beilock, S. (2010). *Choke: What the secrets of the brain reveal about getting it right when you have to*. New York, NY: Free Press.

Bohm, D. (1980). *Wholeness and the implicate order*. New York, NY: Routledge & Kegan Paul.

Bohm, D. (2003). *The essential David Bohm*. (L. Nichol, Ed.) London, England: Routledge.

Briggs, J., & Peat, F. D. (1999). *Seven life lessons of chaos: Spiritual wisdom from the science of change.* New York, NY: HarperCollins.

Csikszentmihalyi, M. (1988). Introduction. In M. Csikszentmihalyi, & I. S. Csikszentmihalyi (Eds.), *Optimal experience: Psychological studies of flow in consciousness.* Cambridge, UK: Cambridge University Press.

Csikszentmihalyi, M. (1990). *Flow: The psychology of optimal experience.* New York, NY: HarperCollins.

Csikszentmihalyi, M. (1993). *The evolving self: A psychology for the third millennium.* New York, NY: HarperPerennial.

Csikszentmihalyi, M. (1997). *Finding flow: The psychology of engagement with everyday life.* New York, NY: Basic Books.

Csikszentmihalyi, M. (2003). *Good business: Leadership, flow, and the making of meaning.* New York, NY: Penguin Group.

Drucker, P. F. (1999). *Management Challenges for the 21st Century.* New York, NY: HarperCollins Publishers, Inc.

Endsley, M. R. (2000). Theoretical underpinnings of situation awareness: A critical review. In M. R. Endsley, & D. J. Garland (Eds.), *Situation awareness analysis and measurement.* Mahwah, NJ: LEA.

Endsley, M. R. (2015, March). Situation awareness: Operationally necessary and scientifically grounded. *Journal of cognitive engineering and decision making, 9*(1), 163-166.

Fave, A. D., & Massimini, F. (1988). Modernization and the changing contexts of flow in work and leisure. In M. Csidszentmihalyi, & I. S. Csikszentmihalyi (Eds.), *Optimal experience: Psychological studies of flow in consciousness* (pp. 193-213). Cambridge, UK: Cambridge University Press.

Ford, D. (2010). *A vision so noble: John Boyd, the OODA Loop, and America's war on terrorism*. Durham, NH: Warbird Books.

Gasaway, R. B. (2009). *Fireground command decision making: Understanding the barriers challenging command situation awareness*. Roseville, MN: Gasaway Consulting Group.

Georgia Smoke Diver. (2016, May 15). *History*. Retrieved from Georgia Smoke Diver: http://www.georgiasmokediver.com

Gladwell, M. (2005). *Blink: The power of thinking without thinking*. New York, NY: Back Bay Books.

Gladwell, M. (2008). *Outliers: The story of success*. New York, NY: Little, Brown.

Glick-Smith, J. L. (2011). The path of the razor's edge: A study of the flow experiences of firefighters (Doctoral dissertation). Available from ProQuest database.

Glick-Smith, J. L. (2015, October 1). *Leading Georgia Smoke Divers*. Retrieved from FirefighterNation: http://www.firerescuemagazine.com/article/special-operations/leading-georgia-smoke-divers

Goerner, S. J., Dyck, R. G., & Lagerroos, D. (2008). *The new science of sustainability: Building a foundation for great change*. Chapel Hill, NC: Triangle Center for Complex Systems.

Goleman, D. (1998). *Working with emotional intelligence*. New York, NY: Bantam Books.

Greenleaf, R. K. (1977). *Servant leadership: A journey into the nature of legitimate power & greatness*. Mahwah, NJ: Paulist Press.

Griffin, D. (2013). *In honor of the Charleston 9: A study of change following tragedy*. Charleston, SC: David Griffin.

Human Performance Consulting, LLC. (2016, May 3). *What We Do.* Retrieved from Welcome to Human Performance Consulting: http://www.hpconsulting.pro/

International Association of Fire Chiefs and National Fire Protection Association. (2006). *Fire officer principles and practice.* Sudbury, MA: Jones & Bartlett.

International Association of Fire Chiefs and U.S. Fire Administration. (2015). *National Safety Culture Change Initiative.* Emmitsburg, MD: Federal Emergency Management Agency.

Jaworski, J. (1998). *Synchronicity: The inner path of leadership.* San Francisco, CA: Berrett-Koehler.

Kahneman, D. (2011). *Thinking, fast and slow.* New York, NY: Farrar, Straus and Giroux.

Klein, G. (1999). *Sources of power: How people make decisions.* Cambridge, MA: MIT Press.

Klein, G. (2003). *The power of intuition: How to use your gut feelings to make better decisions at work.* New York, NY: Currency Books.

Klein, G. (2009). *Streetlights and shadows: Searching for the keys to adaptive decision making.* Cambridge, MA: MIT Press.

Kolditz, T. A. (2007). *In extremis leadership: Leading as if your life depended on it.* San Francisco, CA: Jossey-Bass.

Kopp, D. M., Nikolovska, I., Desiderio, K. P., & Guterman, J. T. (2011). "Relaaax, I remember the recession in the early 1980s...": Organizational storytelling as a crisis management tool. *Human Resource Development Quarterly*, 273-285.

Logan, R. D. (1988). Flow in solitary ordeals. In M. Csikszentmihalyi, & I. S. Csikszentmihalyi (Eds.), *Optimal experience: Psychological studies of flow in consciousness* (pp. 172-182). Cambridge, UK: Cambridge University Press.

Marer, P., Buzady, Z., & Vecsey, Z. (2015). *The missing link discovered*. Los Angeles, CA: ALEAS Simulaions, Inc.

May, R. (1975). *The courage to create*. New York, NY: Norton.

Mischel, W., & DeSmet, A. L. (2000). Self-regulation in the service of conflict resolution. In M. Deutsch, & P. T. Coleman (Eds.), *The handbook of conflict resolution: Theory and practice* (pp. 256-275). San Francisco, CA: John Wiley.

Mullainathan, S., & Shafir, E. (2013). *Scarcity: The new science of having less and how it defines our lives*. New York, NY: Picador.

Peat, F. D. (2008). *Gentle action: Bringing creative change to a turbulent world*. Pari, Grosseto, Italy: Pari Publishing.

Pink, D. H. (2009). *Drive: The surprising truth about what motivates us*. New York, NY: Riverhead Books.

Safer Healthcare. (2016, May 23). *The history of Crew Resource Management*. Retrieved from Safer Healthcare: http://www.saferhealthcare.com/crew-resource-management/what-is-crew-resource-management/

Seligman, M. E. (2002). *Authentic happiness: Using the new positive psychology to realize your potential for lasting fulfillment*. New York, NY: Free Press.

Senge, P. M. (1977). Afterward. In R. K. Greenleaf, *Servant leadership: A journey into the nature of legitimate power & greatness* (pp. 343-359). Mahwah, NJ: Paulist Press.

Smeby, J. L. (2006). *Fire and emergency services administration: Management and leadership practices*. Sudbury, MA: Jones & Bartlett.

Stowell, F. M. (2004). *Chief Officer*. (B. Adams, Ed.) Stillwater, OK: Fire Protection Publications, Oklahoma State University.

Taylor, V. H., & Wolin, S. (2002). *The new normal: How FDNY firefighters are rising to the challenge of life after September 11.* New York, NY: Counseling Service Unit of the FDNY.

Thompson, H. L. (2010). *The stress effect: Why smart leaders make dumb decisions--and what to do about it.* San Francisco, CA: Jossey-Bass.

Thompson, W. I. (1996). *The time falling bodies take to light.* New York, NY: St. Martin's Press.

Wall, D. M. (2016). Decision making in the naturalistic environment of fire and Emergency Services : identifying barriers to situation awareness in fire department company officers (Unpublished doctoral dissertation proposal). Phoenix, AZ: Grand Canyon University.

Watts, A. (1966). *The book: On the taboo against knowing who you are.* New York, NY: Random House.

Watts, A. (2003). *Become what you are.* Boston, MA: Shambhala.

WDCW/DC50TV. (2010). *3rd annual Kyle Wilson 10K walk/run for fitness.* Retrieved April 11, 2010, from WDCW/DC50TV.com: http://www.dc50tv.com/wdcw-kyle-wilson-memorial-story,0,1728270.story

Weick, K. E. (1988). Enacted sensemaking in crisis situations. *Journal of Management Studies,* 305-317.

Weick, K. E. (1995). *Sensemaking in organizations.* Thousand Oaks: Sage.

Weick, K. E., & Sutcliffe, K. M. (2007). *Managing the unexpected: Resilient preformance in an age of uncertainty.* San Francisco, CA: John Wiley.

Index

56875688R00117

Made in the USA
San Bernardino, CA
15 November 2017